Can you positively identify this man?

Can you positively identify this man?

GEORGE INCE and the Barn murder

Peter Cole and Peter Pringle

ANDRE DEUTSCH

First published in 1974 by
André Deutsch Limited
105 Great Russell Street London WC1

Printed in Great Britain by
Butler & Tanner Ltd
Frome and London

ISBN 0 233 96614 5 (Hardback)

ISBN 0 233 96651 X (Paperback)

Contents

Illustrations

Acknowledgements

IT BEGAN as a collection of particularly horrific news stories of the murder at the Barn restaurant in November 1972. Our involvement started when George Ince surrendered to the Essex police three weeks later, and continued when it emerged that Ince had not, as the police at first believed, been responsible for the murder.

We interviewed a large number of people directly connected with the case and it soon became clear that this was much more than a murder inquiry which had led to the prosecution of the wrong man: broader matters of criminal identification and the background to East End crime could not be ignored. We also found it necessary to reconstruct and investigate the silver bullion robbery carried out seven months before the murder.

In addition to published material we have drawn extensively on many preliminary court proceedings and four major trials. But, more importantly, we have drawn on long interviews with the families and friends of the men concerned in the cases. We are indebted to those people, in particular to members of the Ince family, for their forthrightness and patience.

Our thanks also to Robert Patience, who after the personal tragedy of the loss of his wife and the exacting ordeal of the prolonged publicity the case brought him, agreed to be interviewed at length. There were many others whose desire to remain anonymous we have respected.

The Essex police, regrettably, found themselves unable to discuss the case with us, at least up until the time of writing. In reply to a letter of ours the Essex Chief Constable, Mr John Nightingale, wrote on March 19, 1974: 'I am not prepared to discuss it with anyone until such inquiries as are being made into matters related to the case are concluded.'

While we recognize the inevitable gaps left by the

unavailability of the police, we would stress that Supt George Harris of the Essex CID was particularly helpful during the various court proceedings, and we would like to thank him for sparing valuable time to talk to us.

We would also like to thank Harold Evans, editor of the *Sunday Times*, and Alastair Hetherington, editor of the *Guardian*, for allowing us to use material originally collected for publication in those newspapers.

We are grateful to Arthur Davidson and Patrick Milmo for their legal advice, to Lewis Chester who guided us through the initial stages, to Frank Williamson who gave us invaluable advice on the final manuscript, and to three speedy and accurate typists, Sue Dakin, Kathy Stanley and Ros Usher.

The Home Office booklet on Identification Parades reprinted in the Appendix is reproduced by permission of the Controller of Her Majesty's Stationery Office.

And finally our thanks to our editor Faith Evans, who kept the whole project together, gave endless encouragement, and was ever patient when we were miles away working for our newspapers instead of giving in expected manuscripts.

Peter Cole and Peter Pringle

August 1974

Prologue

ON the morning of Monday November 6, 1972, a police car carrying a senior Essex detective turned into the main entrance of Black Notley Hospital, about two miles from the small market town of Braintree. The car went up the tree-lined avenue, passed the clusters of chalet-type wards, and stopped outside the main entrance to the casualty department at the top of the hill. Detective Chief Inspector Derek Wyatt got out of the car and went straight to the intensive care unit. There, recovering from an emergency operation on bullet wounds in her back and stomach, was a pretty twenty-year-old blonde hairdresser called Beverley Patience. She had been shot the previous day by a gunman who had broken into her family home at the Barn, a roadside motel a mile on the other side of Braintree from the hospital.

Beverley's mother Muriel and her father Bob had also been shot. Her mother, who had been unconscious since the shooting, had been transferred to another hospital and was dying slowly from a headwound. Her father had, remarkably, escaped instant death when the bullet aimed at his head had bounced off his skull. Beverley herself had been severely injured. A bullet had entered her back, missed her spine by a fraction of an inch and gone clean through her body. It had sliced through the left lobe of the liver, grazed the main artery, the aorta, and taken a chunk out of her stomach. Wyatt was shown to her bedside knowing just how lucky it was that his chief eye-witness was still alive. The surgeon's report on her wounds had been quite clear: death would have been instantaneous if the track of the bullet had deviated only a fraction to the right.

Wyatt set up a tape-recorder by Beverley's bedside. Although she had responded well to surgery her condition was still regarded as critical, and he was taking this precaution against losing any of her recollections of the shooting. During the next tense minutes Beverley managed to give an astonishingly full description of the incident. The tape-recording is a remarkable document because at the end of the interview the police were in possession of a very detailed and, as it turned out, accurate physical description of the gunman who had burst into the Patience home in the early hours of Guy Fawkes Day. But, in particular, Beverley recalled some distinctive additional evidence. The killer was not a local man, she believed. She had noticed that he spoke with a northern accent, and before he shot her and left her for dead he had told her that he came 'not far from Yorkshire'.

Seven months elapsed before the importance of this vital clue was fully appreciated by the Essex murder squad. During that time the police found a man who fitted enough of Beverley's identification criteria to be charged and tried twice before he was acquitted. That man was George Henry Ince, a building worker from the East End of London. He has an unmistakable cockney accent. The man who, fourteen months after the shooting, was eventually found guilty of the murder was a northerner called John Brook. It is the disturbing events which surrounded the identification of Ince, and allowed his prosecution, which form the core of this book. Identification evidence involving Ince in another case, the silver bullion robbery, which became inextricably tied up with the inquiry into the Barn murder, is also examined in detail. A large number of statements, prepared for the prosecution of the bullion robbers, were in the suspects' possession several months before arrests were made. They made possible a unique insight into the construction of the identification evidence.

When Inspector Wyatt switched on his tape-recorder at Beverley's side, the police knew very little about the raiders. Wyatt simply knew what her father had told him: at about 2 am on the morning of November 5 Beverley had left the Barn restaurant, housed literally in an old converted barn just off the main A120 Braintree to Bishop's Stortford road, to walk the fifty yards to the family's modern three-bedroomed home, known as the Sun Lido House.

First, Wyatt wanted to know why it was she had decided to leave at that hour.

Beverley: I'd been in Majorca for three months and I'd only been back twelve days and I wanted to help Dad working down the Barn this winter and then get a job in Majorca again next summer. I got tired by two o'clock and I wanted to go home early.

Wyatt: Oh, I see. Now when had you last been over the house?

Beverley: I went from the house to the restaurant about 8 o'clock because I was going to help with the cloakroom, then afterwards I went back again because there was someone in to do that. I had something to eat over the house and I suppose I came back about nine, a quarter past nine. But Mum was still in the house after I had gone.

Wyatt: So she was the last one in the house?

Beverley: I would think so.

Wyatt: Now when you left the Barn at about 2 o'clock you were with Mum?

Beverley: Yes.

Wyatt: Now, in detail as far as you can, tell me exactly what happened.

Beverley: We went in the kitchen first, in the restaurant, to cut some food for the dog, and then we went into the house by the front door – with my key.

Wyatt: Were there any lights on?

Beverley: Yes, we always leave lights on over there anyway, two in the lounge and I can't remember if there was one in the . . . yes, one in the porch. I had the dog meat: I went into the kitchen and switched the light on . . . and screamed because I saw them.

Wyatt: It was in darkness?

Beverley: Yes.

Wyatt: And you turned the light on?

Beverley: Yes and saw them.

Wyatt: Where were they standing?

Beverley: If you walk in our kitchen there's a door and a tall cupboard, one was standing so he could get out round the table. The other one was over by the cooker.

Wyatt: What were they doing?

Beverley: They stood there. I screamed and threw the dog's meat in the air. I tried to push Mum back and close the door, but they opened it and they had guns.

Wyatt: They had guns?

Beverley: Well, the blond one had a gun, the other one had a briefcase with his arm in it, so I presumed he had a gun.

Wyatt: Then what happened?

Beverley: Mum went a bit hysterical and I tried to calm her down. They told us to go into the front room and sit down. I tried to calm Mum down and I asked the dark-haired one to get her a drink of water and she kept asking them: 'What do you want? What do you want?'

Wyatt: Had they said anything to you at this stage?

Beverley: They said: 'If you keep quiet and it goes all right no one's going to get hurt.'

Wyatt: Who said that?

Beverley: The blond one. The dark one hardly spoke at all.

Wyatt: Before we go any further I want you to describe them to me. First off I want you to describe what you call the blond one.

Beverley: Very very sandy blond hair.

Wyatt: Now wait a minute, hold on. Describe the blond one first. How old was he?

Beverley: About early thirties. I couldn't pinpoint it. You know, early thirties, twenty-nine, thirty or thirty-one.

Wyatt: Right, how tall was he?

Beverley: About five foot eight.

Wyatt: What sort of build?

Beverley: Slim.

Wyatt: Definitely slim?

Beverley: Yes.

Wyatt: Now start at the top. What about his hair. What colour was it?

Beverley: Sandy blond.

Wyatt: Sandy blond. Blonder than yours?

Beverley: Yes.

Wyatt: Much fairer than yours?

Beverley: Yes.

Wyatt: And definitely blond as opposed to fair?

Beverley: Oh, yes.

Wyatt: Now, what style was it?

Beverley: From what I can remember it was combed forward from the crown, but it was receding a lot here and it was very short.

Wyatt: Very short?

Beverley: What I call short.

Wyatt: Soldier short, not long.

Beverley: Not long. But no sideboards.

Wyatt: Was there anything particular about his face?

Beverley: Very blue eyes, a bit of a sallow complexion.

Wyatt: Anything about his nose or mouth?

Beverley: Very even white teeth.

Wyatt: Anything particular about his lips or mouth?

Beverley: I think his lips tended to be a little on the full side.

Wyatt: What about his chin?

Beverley: I can't remember.

Wyatt: Any scars or marks?

Beverley: Not facially, not that I can remember.

Wyatt: Right, now what about his dress, try and think as far as you can about what he was wearing.

Beverley: I'm a bit muddled about this. I think he had a beige/stony kind of mac on. With the collar turned up. I can't remember what colour trousers. I think old-fashioned brown shoes, or what I call old-fashioned. Not lace-up. Just had a kind of buckle on the side. And a chiselly toe.

Wyatt: Yes. Now what sort of voice? He was the one who spoke to you, was he?

Beverley: Yes. He had a very, very, slight Yorkshire accent I believe, because Mum said to him 'Where do you come from, Yorkshire?' and he just grinned and said: 'Not far off.'

Wyatt: Now think about the other one, the dark-haired one, and start again exactly as we did before. How old do you think he was?

Beverley: Twenty-seven to twenty-eight.

Wyatt: About what height?

Beverley: Very tall: I would say about six foot one to two.

Wyatt: Much taller than the other one.

Beverley: Yes.

Wyatt: What about his build?

Beverley: Slim, broad shoulders, but slim waist.

Wyatt: What about his hair?

Beverley: Very dark brown. He had a side parting and over. I think he had a bit of sideboard. It [his hair] was just beginning to flick up a little at the back, not much.

Wyatt: What about his face?

Beverley: I'm not really sure about that. He had brown eyes. And I think he had a slim face. I'm not sure if it was him or the blond one, but one of them had a mole on one of the cheeks. Yes, somewhere up here I think. (Beverley indicates somewhere underneath the eye.)

Wyatt: What about his mouth?

Beverley: I can't remember that at all.

Wyatt: Anything about his chin that was outstanding enough for you to remember it now?

Beverley: I'm not sure.

Wyatt: Now let's concentrate on his dress then.

Beverley: He had a suit on, a kind of grey tweed, not a heavy one, a light one. It was kind of, not as dark as yours. It was more of a white background with grey and black bits in it.

Wyatt: What about collar and tie or anything like that?

Beverley: He had a scarf, tartan-coloured, beige and blue in it.

Wyatt: When you say scarf, do you mean winter scarf?

Beverley: Yes, not a long one.

Wyatt: Not one of these casual ones?

Beverley: No. It was a scarf.

Wyatt: Not a gypsy scarf? It was a definite scarf?

Beverley: Yes. And I believe he had a maroon tie or a darkish one, and a blue shirt and a suit that didn't fit all that well. It was a bit big.

Wyatt: How about the shoes?

Beverley: I can't remember, I can only remember one pair of brown shoes that were old-fashioned and I think the blond one had them on, but I can't swear to it.

Wyatt: All right. Go back to the blond one. We discussed his mackintosh. What about his collar and tie?

Beverley: I can't remember.

Wyatt: Not that he didn't have one. Just that you're not sure.

Beverley: I think it was almost definite that he did have a collar and tie, but I can't remember.

Wyatt: You can't remember. Right now I wanted to get what you said to them and what they said to you, where you sat, the state you were in, the state they were in, and, in particular, all the little snippets of conversation that they may have had with you. You see it's extremely important when we come to build up a picture and, in fact, of getting hold of them, you see?

Beverley: Yes.

Wyatt: So, you've gone to the kitchen, they have ushered you out, the blond one has got the gun.

Beverley: Yes.

Wyatt: Was it in any way disguised in the kitchen? Did he cover it or hide it?

Beverley: No.

Wyatt: It was quite open and it was pointed at you?

Beverley: Yes. And they both had black leather gloves on.

Wyatt: This is our girl. Now, then, black leather gloves. Definitely both of them?

Beverley: Definitely.

Wyatt: They took you, they ushered you into the lounge?

Beverley: Yes.

Wyatt: Who was the first in the ushering, was it the blond or the black-haired one?

Beverley: I think the dark one stood by the arch in the front room and the blond one told us to sit down and Mum was sat at the far end of the settee. I sat next to her. The blond one sat opposite there, in the chair by the window and the other one stood by the arch. Mum was going a bit hysterical.

Wyatt: Yes, right.

Beverley: So I asked the dark one to get her a glass of water and he got her one.

Wyatt: From the kitchen?

Beverley: Yes, and then the blond one kept telling her to shut up.

Wyatt: What exactly did he say?

Beverley: He said: 'Keep your voice down because this will be silent.' And he had the cushion and the gun behind the cushion. He picked up the cushion. I then tried to calm Mum down and I said to them: 'What would you do if you got caught?' And they said: 'There's a very slim chance of that at all.' Mum kept saying you want the money and everything. The blond one asked me where the key to the safe was and I said it wasn't kept at the house. If it was anywhere it would be over at the restaurant. And then Mummy said: 'Can't I go to bed?' They said: 'Not unless you want to be tied up.' So I said: 'No, stay here.' Mum said to him: 'Where do you come from, you've got a slight Yorkshire accent?' He said: 'Not far off.' I said: 'How much do you get for armed robbery nowadays?' and I've forgotten what he said now. Thirty years would he have said? Or twenty?

Wyatt: He could have done. Is that what he said?

Beverley: I think he said it was about twenty.

Wyatt: Yes.

Beverley: And I said: 'Well, you won't come out much under fifty then.' He just grinned. That's all that was said. Then Dad came in.

Wyatt continued his questioning right through the shooting, and Beverley's stark recollections of the horror of it all are recorded later, but the purpose here is to concentrate on her first impressions of the raiders. Importantly, Beverley had given a previous description of the two men to a nurse at the Black Notley, Susan Shepherd. She had stayed at Beverley's bedside until she was taken into the operating theatre the day before, a matter of hours after the shooting. Beverley gave Nurse Shepherd less detailed but exactly similar descriptions of the two men and she included the distinctive piece of evidence – that the gunman spoke with a Yorkshire accent.

1-Murder at the Barn

JOHN BROOK and Nicholas de Clare Johnson met, as arranged, on the morning of November 4, 1972, in London. They went to Liverpool Street station where they caught a train to Chelmsford, a journey of about forty minutes. In Chelmsford they caught a bus to Braintree, eleven miles away, arriving there at lunchtime. There were twelve hours to kill before they could complete their business at the Barn Restaurant, on the west side of Braintree. They believed that the Barn's owner, Bob Patience, had a great deal of money in his safe, and they intended to steal that money before they returned to London.

The two men's approach to the crime lacked professionalism. Professional burglars do not travel to their destination by train, bus and on foot, with so little thought for their getaway, nor do they need to ask directions to the house they plan to rob. But, on the other hand, amateurs do not carry guns and John Brook had in his pocket a small Beretta automatic pistol. It was loaded.

Brook had been a criminal for most of his life. Born in Leeds in 1943 – his voice still carries perceptible traces of a Yorkshire accent – he had had his first confrontation with the police at the age of fifteen. He had been in an approved school, Borstal and prisons, mostly for shopbreaking and theft. But in 1970 he was convicted of a violent crime: assault causing actual bodily harm. A homosexual made advances to him, and Brook hit him hard with an iron bar, then hit him again as he lay moaning on the floor. He was sentenced to three years in prison, much of which he spent in Dartmoor.

Brook was a thin man with high cheekbones, a high forehead and receding hairline. His eyebrows slanted upwards away from the bridge of his nose, but his dominant facial feature was his eyes. They were steely blue, staring and penetrating, and emphasized his cold, sinister appearance. One of the eyes was not his own: it was a glass eye which was, if anything, bluer than the other. Early in his life Brook had had an ocular infection. The disease was not properly treated, and as a result he eventually lost the eye.

He had always found it hard to make friends and had a reputation for being solitary and uncommunicative. Johnson was one of the few people with whom he achieved anything like a friendship, although even this appears to have been based as much as anything on Johnson's prolonged efforts to understand him. Johnson saw himself as something of an amateur psychologist, and though he feared Brook in many ways he also found him fascinating and believed he could help him. It was a strange and complex relationship, which had begun some years earlier in the Grendon Underhill psychiatric prison in Buckinghamshire.

Nicholas de Clare Johnson was a very different type from his partner. He had boyish, impudent good looks and an extrovert character. He was a successful womanizer, a lover of fast cars and the good life. He was also a regular church-goer. But his life, like Brook's, had been one of crime. He was an illegitimate child, born on Christmas Day 1943. Originally named Michael Steiner, he spent his early years in an orphanage until being adopted when still a small child. He took the surname of his adoptive parents, Johnson. They called him Nicholas; the 'de Clare' was his own idea, added after he left home. He thought it gave a touch of distinction.

Johnson had thirteen convictions, none of them for violent crimes. Usually they were connected with cars. He had stolen cars, driven them uninsured, driven them without a licence. His most recent conviction had been in 1970 when he was jailed for four years for obtaining a car by deception. His selection for the prison hostel scheme while he was at Albany prison on the Isle of Wight had resulted in his being transferred to Pentonville prison in London.

In fact on the day Johnson went to Braintree with Brook he was still officially serving his prison sentence. The hostel scheme is designed to help prisoners serving sentences of four years or more to reintegrate into the community during the last few months before their release. They can go out of the prison during the day to do a normal job of work for normal pay. Brook had been selected for the same scheme at Pentonville while he was in Dartmoor. His sentence had ended three weeks before that November 4.

A bonus in the hostel scheme is that the prisoner taking part in it can go away for the occasional weekend. He signs out of prison on a Friday evening, leaving the address where he will be staying the weekend, and must be back in prison by Sunday night. Johnson had signed out of Pentonville at 5 pm the previous day and had left the address of a friend of his in Romsey, Hampshire.

But he knew he would not be spending the Saturday in Hampshire. The plans for the robbery, such as they were, were already laid. Brook and Johnson had been pleased to meet again in Pentonville. Although it had been some years since they had seen each other, their friendship was quickly renewed. Johnson enjoyed being able to study Brook once again. He later told the police, when he was confessing to being at the Barn on that November night: 'No one could get close to him. He seemed so remote and isolated. I am torn between protecting John Brook from himself and the protection of innocent people. He seemed to be lost not knowing himself. I suppose I recognized the psychopathic tendencies.'

Brook and Johnson had planned the Barn robbery while they were working for the same furniture firm on the hostel scheme. They were not the first to have the idea. The Barn was a common talking-point among the criminal fraternity: it was one of those places which was 'known about', and in London prisons and in certain pubs small groups of men discussed the possibility of robbing it. The Barn was popular among East Enders looking for nights out. Patience himself was well-known because he had once owned a club in the East End. It was no secret that on Friday and Saturday nights the Barn did good business and that the takings were kept in a safe over the weekend until they could be banked. It was also thought that Patience kept rather more than two nights' takings in his safe. The 'Barn job' was marked as worth doing, and it was being offered around. Patience himself was aware of this.

Brook and Johnson had heard the talk, but it seems that they were not carrying out the job 'for' anybody. Theirs was a

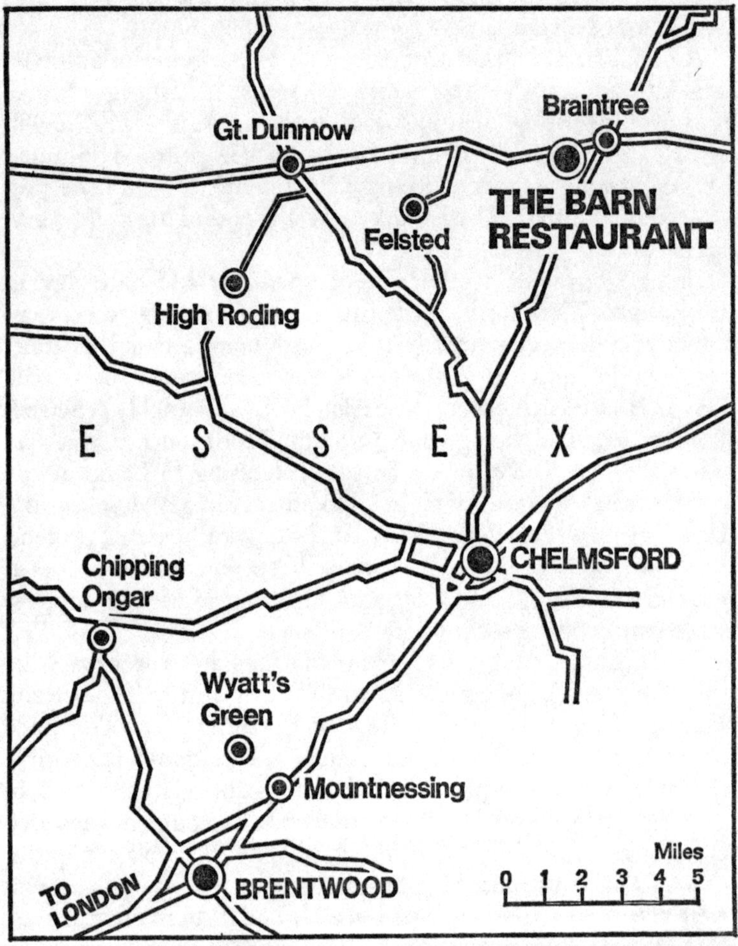

free-lance enterprise. They decided on a date soon after Brook's release. It was easy for Johnson to be available: he could sign out for the weekend, and as long as he was back in prison on Sunday night no suspicions would be aroused.

So at lunchtime on that Saturday November 4, the two men stood in the middle of Braintree, by the market, where the bus had dropped them. Neither had been to the town before, and as they had no idea where the Barn was they decided to ask for directions. They approached an elderly man called Jonathan Ridley who was waiting for his wife outside Fosters' men's clothing shop. They asked him the way to Rayne Road. 'What are you looking for?' asked Ridley. 'The swimming baths,' said Johnson confidently. Ridley was puzzled for a moment. What swimming baths? Then he remembered the old public baths beside the Barn restaurant. They had been out of use for several years; the changing quarters were rotting and falling down and there was no water in the pool. But the men had said Rayne Road, so that must be the pool to which they were referring. 'That's a long way down Rayne Road,' he said, 'at the bottom of the hill.' The two men thanked him and set off.

They walked to the Barn and had a brief look around. There was the sprawling, old whitewashed barn, converted into a restaurant and bars, its gaudy neon signs giving an impression more of a mid-West American motel than a restaurant in a quiet Essex market town. They saw the motel units which Patience was building at the back of the Barn. They saw, too, the Sun Lido House, the Patiences' private home, about fifty yards away from the main restaurant building. They had plenty of time on their hands until the robbery, so they got on a bus and returned to Chelmsford. *The Italian Job* was showing at the cinema; they couldn't resist seeing it.

George Ince got up soon after nine on the morning of November 4. He was living in a caravan, which he owned, on a site just outside Whitstable in north Kent. He made a cup of tea for himself and for Frankie Sims, a friend who was staying in the caravan with him. He was in a good mood. He liked Saturdays; it was the day he usually went to London to visit his girlfriend.

Ince had been living out of London for much of the past six months. He knew the police wanted him for questioning about the hijacking of a lorry carrying a large amount of silver bullion, but his reaction had not been that of a man on the run: he had been living in the caravan quite openly, using his real name, making regular trips to London. Ince was born a cockney. He came from a large East End family and had two brothers and five sisters. He had a small criminal record, but not for anything very serious; his last conviction had been more than ten years before. He had known several of the more celebrated East End criminals. One of his sisters says of him: 'George is no angel; he's been around a bit.'

Sims and Ince drank their tea and then went into Whitstable, where they met another friend, Charles (Chic) Matthews. Ince backed a couple of horses in a betting shop, and his mood improved further when one of them won. The three men went into a restaurant for lunch and afterwards had a sauna bath. Feeling refreshed, Ince collected some clean shirts from the laundry at about 4 o'clock and drove his Ford Escort back to the caravan. He cooked himself ham and eggs and watched television. Then he prepared himself for his night out. He shaved and changed into a grey suit and mauve shirt with a blue and mauve tie. As usual he took a lot of trouble getting ready. He was very fussy about his appearance, liked clothes and spent a lot of money on them.

He got into the Escort and drove the fifty-odd miles to London, stopping in Bexleyheath to phone his sister, Rose Threadwell, who lived with her husband Jim in a council house in Manor Park. He was very close to Rose. When he was living in London she used to clean his flat, which was just round the corner from her house, and mother him in the way of an elder sister. Since he had been away Rose had regularly paid his rent and done odd favours for him, like taking suits to the cleaners. That was why Ince was phoning. Could Rose meet him behind the Poplar Hospital and bring one of his clean suits? Mrs Threadwell and her husband Jim drove in their van to the back of the hospital. When they pulled up Ince got out of the Escort and crossed to the Threadwells' van. The three of them chatted for almost half an hour, then Ince took the suit, kissed his sister goodbye, and gave her £2 so that she could buy her children some fireworks. Since Guy Fawkes Day fell on a Sunday in 1972 most people were celebrating on the

Saturday night. Ince drove off to see his girlfriend.

At about 8.30 that evening Mrs Doris Grey was letting off fireworks for her small daughter at the bottom of the block of council flats in Poplar where they lived. It was getting cold and she took her back upstairs to bed. Mrs Grey was looking forward to George's visit; she admitted now that she loved him, although she was still married. It had been a fraught romance, which both she and Ince had at first tried to keep secret. Her husband was Charlie Kray, the elder brother of the Kray twins, Ronnie and Reggie. He was in Maidstone prison, serving a ten-year sentence he had been given in 1968 for his part in the disposal of Jack 'The Hat' McVitie's body. As Charlie's wife she had always been known as Dolly. Since 1969 she had changed her name by deed poll – rather less radically than she might have done – to Grey.

Shortly before 9 pm Ince arrived. Mrs Grey made some tea and the two of them talked and watched television for the rest of the evening. Some time around 11 they went to bed. At about 9 the following morning Ince drove back to his caravan at Whitstable.

At about the same time as Ince was going to bed, John Brook and Nicholas Johnson caught the last bus from Chelmsford to Braintree. They bought some chips and ate them as they walked along Rayne Road towards the Barn. When they arrived there they decided it was too early to break in, so they waited in a field beside the restaurant.

The neon sign outside the Barn claimed: 'Every night is party night', and that Saturday was no exception. The restaurant and bars were thronging with people who had come from all over south Essex and the East End. The band was playing and the drinks were flowing. Bob Patience, who likes to describe himself as 'mine host', was being just that, scurrying busily around, checking that everything was going smoothly, even at one point climbing on to the stage to sing 'Happy Birthday' to one of the guests. The three hundred or so who had paid £5 for their tickets were enjoying the cabaret, starring comedian Ted Rogers. Patience's wife Muriel and his son David were hard at work, together with his daughter Beverley. She had just returned from three months in Majorca, where Patience owned a flat.

Muriel Patience was a kindly, motherly woman, devoted to her children and popular with her friends. She participated in all her husband's business projects, happily joining in the enormous amount of work involved in building up and running a restaurant. She was as tall as her husband, had blonde hair, and dressed neatly and conventionally. She was particularly close to Beverley.

Patience was at his happiest when he saw his creation, the Barn, packed with people enjoying themselves. In ten years he had transformed the place from a small roadside transport café into a flourishing nightspot. It was now worth anything up to £500,000 and it was still growing. The motel units behind the restaurant were almost built and Patience saw his business going from strength to strength.

The Barn would not be everybody's choice of a nightspot, but it appealed to enough people to keep Bob Patience wealthy and happy. He had stamped his character all over it. The original café had been extended in all directions so that the Barn now fully lived up to its name. It bristled with oak beams, both genuine and ersatz, and almost every square inch of wall space was covered with horse-brasses and the heads of stuffed animals. Old oil-lamps hung from the ceiling. But Patience's pride and joy was the Cavalier Bar, and as a lover of gimmickry he was proudest of its roof. At the touch of a button two huge sections of the ceiling slid slowly back, under electric power, to expose the night sky above. 'It helps to clear the fog,' Patience explains to astounded visitors. There was another unmistakable Patience touch in the brickwork of the bar itself. Set into a crevice in the brick facing the bar was a plaster cast of a hand, beneath which was inscribed: 'The hand of Patience who designed and built this bar.'

Patience was the complete extrovert: a short, plump, busy man who liked nothing better than to talk about himself and his life. His visiting card epitomized him. A postcard-sized colour print, it showed a photograph of him in evening dress holding up a white board headed 'Never admit defeat'. Underneath were listed 'just a few of the rough spots in the life of Abraham Lincoln'. There were fifteen items: among them electoral failures, nervous breakdowns, business disasters. Patience identified very strongly with the sentiments. At the bottom of the card was written: 'With the compliments of mine host, Bob Patience.'

'Never admit defeat' was a theme Patience returned to often. He had been a gunner in RAF bombers during the war until he was invalided out in 1943. He immediately went into business with his brother Frank. They sold reject china, and then second-hand furniture, most of it damaged in the blitz. After that they sold firewood and logs. In the fifties the Patience brothers won a contract from Joe Lyons to produce 250,000 lollipop sticks a week: East End housewives helped out in their spare time.

In 1959 Bob Patience moved into the nightclub business for the first time. The Ashurst Club in Ilford was short of money for its Christmas fund and Patience made up the amount needed. The club soon became his and he immediately set about stamping it with his own showman's personality. He had paid a visit to the western United States and believed a cowboy theme would go down well in East London. He renamed the club the Ranch House, fitted it out like a log cabin, and called himself the marshal. He used to strut around the club in a big cowboy hat and cowboy clothes, with cap guns in his holsters.

The Ranch House became a famous spot for East Enders, visited by many celebrities. But in 1961 there was an ugly incident. A man called Ronald Coomber died after being set upon and kicked in the throat by a group of men in the Ranch House car park. Shortly after this Patience was picked up by a group of gangsters who drove him to an address in the East End and told him to 'have a word' with everybody at the club that night who had seen the assault on Coomber. According to Patience, the man who issued this warning was brandishing a gun.

Four men were later charged with Coomber's murder, but they were all acquitted. Patience decided to move on. He sold the Ranch House to Billy Butlin, and bought the Barn.

The band was still playing at the Barn that Saturday night when Patience took a few of his staff home in his bronze Mercedes. It was 1.30 am. At about that time Brook and Johnson crept round the back of Sun Lido House. They clambered up to Beverley's bedroom window and entered the house. As they walked through the bedroom they saw Beverley's large teddy-bear lying on the bed. They began to search the house for the keys to the safe they had found in the hall.

At around 2 am Muriel and Beverley Patience, tired after a busy night, decided they would go home to bed. The dancing was still going on but people were now beginning to leave: the two women could be spared. They went into the kitchen to collect some food for their dog Kipper, and walked the fifty yards to Sun Lido House. There were still several coaches parked outside, their drivers chatting together. Two of them, Cyril Mayo and William Isted, noticed Muriel and Beverley crossing the car park.

All descriptions of what followed in Sun Lido House are based on the recollections of Beverley, and later of Bob Patience. The account of Brook and Johnson's retreat from the Barn is based on what Johnson told the police.

Beverley opened the front door with her key and carried the dog food down the hall to the kitchen. Her mother followed close behind. Beverley switched on the kitchen light and immediately let out a scream at the sight of Brook and Johnson, who had been standing there in the darkness. Brook was holding a gun. Beverley dropped the dog food and, retreating backwards out of the kitchen, tried to close the door. But Brook had stepped across the room and stopped her. She bumped into her mother, who was already in a state of hysteria.

'Be quiet, it's not you I want,' said Brook. 'If there is no trouble no one will get hurt.'

Beverley went up to her mother to try to calm her, and then both women were told to go into the lounge. They sat down side by side on the settee. Mrs Patience was still hysterical and Brook told her to shut up. Muriel Patience kept asking: 'What do you want?'

Brook sat down on a chair opposite the settee and picked up a pink velvet cushion which he held in front of the gun. 'Be quiet,' he said. 'Because if I have to use it it won't make any noise.' Brook asked Beverley where the keys to the safe were and she told him that they were over in the restaurant. Mrs Patience, trembling with fear, blurted: 'You work hard all your life for this money and then someone like you comes and takes it all.'

In the coach park William Isted, the driver, remarked to another driver that there were men in Sun Lido House. The sitting room curtains were slightly parted and from where he was sitting in the coach Isted could see a man's shoulder through the gap. He thought they must be friends of the Patiences.

At about 2.15 am, Bob Patience, back from delivering his staff, decided to take a walk round the back of the restaurant to the new motel buildings. The band was still playing and he wanted to check how much of the noise could be heard in the bedrooms where guests would soon be sleeping. On the way he called in at Sun Lido House. Beverley heard his footsteps. Brook told her and Mrs Patience to keep quiet.

Patience walked in through the front door, passed the dog lying quietly in the hall, and then opened the lounge door. He was confronted by Brook, holding the pink cushion up in front of his face with the gun behind it. 'What goes on?' asked Patience calmly.

'Don't do anything, Bob, they've got a gun,' shouted his wife. Brook motioned Patience to sit on a chair beyond the settee where his wife and daughter sat. He then sat down himself opposite the settee, and asked Patience for the key to the safe. Patience took a gamble. He knew there was a key in the room in which he was sitting, but he told Brook that the key was over at the Barn, and that anyway there was no money in the safe.

The band in the restaurant was playing 'The party's over'. Patience said: 'You can hear the music. There are cabaret artistes over there who have to be paid and I always pay them; so in a very short time somebody will come looking for me.' He said the keys were in the restaurant and he would take Brook there with him if he promised no harm would come to Muriel or Beverley. 'Don't be a bleeding fool, Bob, I want the keys to the safe,' Brook replied. He asked for the keys several more times, but still Patience maintained that they were in the restaurant.

Muriel Patience, who had not spoken for some time, looked up in surprise. 'You mentioned my husband's name,' she said. Bob Patience was also surprised; he had never seen the man before. But Brook offered no explanation. Instead he deepened the mystery by remarking: 'This is a family concern.' Then he raised the gun, keeping it behind the cushion, and pointed it first at Mrs Patience, then at Beverley. He moved it from one to the other, saying in a hushed voice: 'Your wife or your daughter?' There was a pause.

'Your wife, I think.' There was a bang, and Mrs Patience slumped forward. The bullet had hit her just above the right temple. She screamed. Patience leapt to his feet crying: 'You've murdered my wife.' Brook remained impassive, still repeating that he wanted the keys to the safe. The keys were, in fact, in a bowl on the mantelpiece, as Patience had known all along. He had been confident that his apparent fearlessness and his contemptuous attitude to the gunman, in contrast with his wife's hysterics, would persuade Brook that he was not going to give in. But the sight of his wife bleeding and moaning on the settee convinced him, too late, that he would have to cooperate. He crossed the room to the mantelpiece and held up the keys.

Brook was right behind him holding the gun as he went out into the hall to the safe and opened it. Patience took out a bag containing his wife's jewellery and put it down to one side of the safe. He took out two Barclay's Bank bags containing some cash, cheques and credit slips, and threw them at Brook's feet.

Brook said nothing as Patience put the jewellery bag back in the safe. He didn't look in the safe; he made no effort to look for the secret compartment where Patience had concealed more than £7000. Brook ordered Patience back into the lounge.

Mrs Patience was delirious. Johnson, who had said nothing and had just been sitting quietly in the room throughout the episode with the safe keys, went to the kitchen to fetch a towel. He and Beverley tried to halt the bleeding. Brook and Patience came back into the lounge. Patience looked at his wife. Blood was coming from her mouth as well as from the bullet wound. He turned to Brook: 'You've killed her, you bastard.' Brook went up to Mrs Patience and took a look at her wound. 'She'll be all right,' he said casually.

Brook muttered some instructions to Johnson, who left the room and came back with a plastic clothes line and two ties. Brook told him to tie up Patience and Beverley. Patience was pleading with Brook to call an ambulance for his wife, but Brook said nothing and stood over Patience and his daughter while Johnson tied them up and gagged them. Both were lying face down on the floor. Mrs Patience, who had been lying across the settee, fell forward on to the floor. Brook then knelt over Beverley. 'No don't,' she cried. Without warning he fired one shot through the cushion into her back. She screamed. Brook crossed to Patience, put the cushion against the side of his head, and fired another shot. He picked up the keys to David Patience's blue Volkswagen estate car from the mantelpiece and hurried out of Sun Lido House. He got into the car next to Johnson.

Miraculously Patience had twitched his head at the moment Brook fired the shot at him; he escaped with a relatively minor injury to his ear when the bullet aimed directly into his head bounced off his skull. As soon as they were alone in the room he rolled over towards the intercom which connected the house with the restaurant. He managed to work a hand free and pushed every intercom button.

David had been working in the restaurant throughout the grotesque events in the house. He picked up the receiver, and realized immediately from his father's voice that something terrible had happened. He ran out of the restaurant and across the gravel towards the house. Brook and Johnson were pulling away in his Volkswagen; Johnson was behind the wheel. The car brushed against one of the coach drivers, Ronald Lea, who was standing in the coach park with his back to it. Lea yelled: 'You mad bastard,' as the car accelerated across the yard. As David ran across the gravel he glanced at the car.

The Volkswagen swung left out of the Barn car park and headed down the Dunmow Road. Brook and Johnson abandoned it after a few miles and took to the fields. It was nearly 3 am. After they had walked for some time Johnson asked Brook about the shots. 'There are no witnesses now,' Brook replied. 'I shot Beverley through her back to her heart and I shot the man in the head.'

Johnson was angry. 'You fool, what have you involved me in? It was burglary and you have turned it into mass murder. Why the gun, John, why?'

Brook laughed. 'You are involved, it's too late now. You want to be careful because I still have the gun.' It was a long, wet night. The two men walked for miles along a disused railway track. It was approaching dawn on Sunday morning when they came across an old pillbox and went inside. They sat down and divided up the money they had stolen. It amounted to only £200 each. They burnt the cheques and a map they had stolen, and buried the ashes. They continued walking and eventually came to a road, where they hitched a lift to the outskirts of Chelmsford in a Land-Rover with some workmen. After they had been dropped they bought a pint of milk from a milk-float. They hitched another lift into the centre of Chelmsford, and returned to the railway station where they had arrived the previous day. The police had been hunting for them for some six hours when they boarded a train for London.

2 · The great bullion robbery

On Tuesday May 2, 1972, six months before the Barn shootings, two women detectives from Scotland Yard's Regional Crime Squad, Sergeant Judy Andrews and Constable Margaret Cooper, were sitting in an unmarked police car in the Essex town of Goodmayes. It was 7.30 in the morning. The car was stationary, its engine switched off, and Judy Andrews was in the driving seat. Their instructions were to keep an eye on 24 Alloa Road, the home of a market trader called Anthony Sillett, known to his friends as Golly.

The police have never revealed why Sillett was being kept under observation. The two detectives had been trailing him for a week – it was 'routine surveillance' being carried out 'as a result of information received'. But the police never divulged just what that information was or what exactly routine surveillance amounted to.

Judy Andrews and Margaret Cooper sat quietly in their car and watched the front door of No. 24 for an hour and a quarter before anything happened. Then the door opened and Sillett came out. He got into his Sunbeam Imp and drove off. Judy Andrews started the car and followed. Sillett drove into the East End, stopped outside a house in Forest Gate, and went inside. A few moments later he came out again, this time with another man. The two of them got into a large Ford and drove off.

The two detectives, who had pulled up well clear of the house, shadowed the Ford at a distance. It followed an odd course, round one block, round another, never stopping, and eventually returned to the original Forest Gate house. The two men went inside again. It was 10.35 am and the detectives called off their surveillance and drove away from the area. Once again, it has never been explained why, if they were watching Sillett, they abandoned their vigil at that moment, particularly in view of the events which were to follow that day.

As the detectives began their surveillance outside Golly Sillett's house in Goodmayes, Raymond Kerley was arriving at work in Holywell Lane, near Liverpool Street station, from his home in Ashford, Kent. He was a security officer for a firm called MAT Transport, travelling beside the driver in the cab, responsible for the safety of valuable loads. He had left home early that morning because he had been told his work would involve an early start, but he did not yet know what the job would be.

MAT Transport was a large business divided into two sections: one was responsible for collecting and delivering payrolls, the other transported bullion and other valuable loads. Kerley's work usually took him to airports or seaports, and he would travel with a driver and up to two other men. At the Holywell Lane depot he was given the collection and delivery notes which told him what his job would be that day. He was to travel in a lorry delivering a load of silver bullion to Parkeston Quay, part of the Essex seaport of Harwich.

At about 7.45 am a huge articulated container truck was driven into the depot. It was a long vehicle with a dark-blue tractor unit and a silver container behind. This was the truck in which Kerley would be going to Harwich. It was driven by a man called Tony Evans, whom Kerley did not know well but remembered from one previous journey to Harwich. Kerley joined Evans in the cab and they drove over the river to a firm of silver brokers in Tooley Street, Southwark, to collect 643 ingots of silver bullion valued at almost £400,000. They reached the silver brokers at about 8.15. Evans edged the lorry into the loading bay and then went off to breakfast with another MAT employee who had arrived to help transfer the silver.

Kerley stayed with the lorry. He closed the rear doors of the container and applied four seals, recording their numbers on the company receipt. Evans and the other man, called John, returned from breakfast and the three of them started loading the silver ingots, weighing about twenty tons, into the container from the pallets on which they were stacked. It was hard work, and the men paused halfway through their loading for a cup of tea. Kerley counted the bars into the container. He was responsible for making sure they were all there. When the loading was complete he closed and sealed the container side door they had been using. Then he realized he had forgotten to seal the weight list inside the container with the bullion, so he broke off the seals, put the list inside, and resealed the container. Evans drove the truck away from the loading bay, parked it, and went back to the café with John. Kerley stayed with the lorry. It was about 11 am.

One of the other lorries in the yard was fitted with a two-way radio and Kerley went across to it and called up headquarters to tell them the loading was finished and he and Evans would be setting off for Harwich very soon. Evans returned from the café, and just before 11.15 the truck with its £400,000 load rolled out of the yard. It was on its own. There was no escort, no radio contact with base. The Essex police, through whose territory the lorry would be passing for most of its journey, were told nothing about it. Kerley, the security guard, carried no weapon. To anybody who knew of the journey in advance the transporter was a relatively easy target. Several men did know – and long enough in advance to make meticulous plans and preparations for what was to be one of the biggest robberies Essex had ever known.

There was no discussion about the route to be taken; both Evans and Kerley had done that run before and the route was always the same. They drove out of Tooley Street, crossed the Thames at Tower Bridge, and out through the East End along Whitechapel Road and Leytonstone High Road until they joined the North Circular Road. That led the lorry out to the main A12, the trunk road which runs from London through the East Anglian towns of Chelmsford, Colchester and Ipswich to Great Yarmouth. Evans and Kerley were out on the main road; it was an easy drive from then on. They relaxed and chatted.

By 12.15 they were approaching the Brentwood bypass. Just short of the village of Mountnessing there is a roundabout

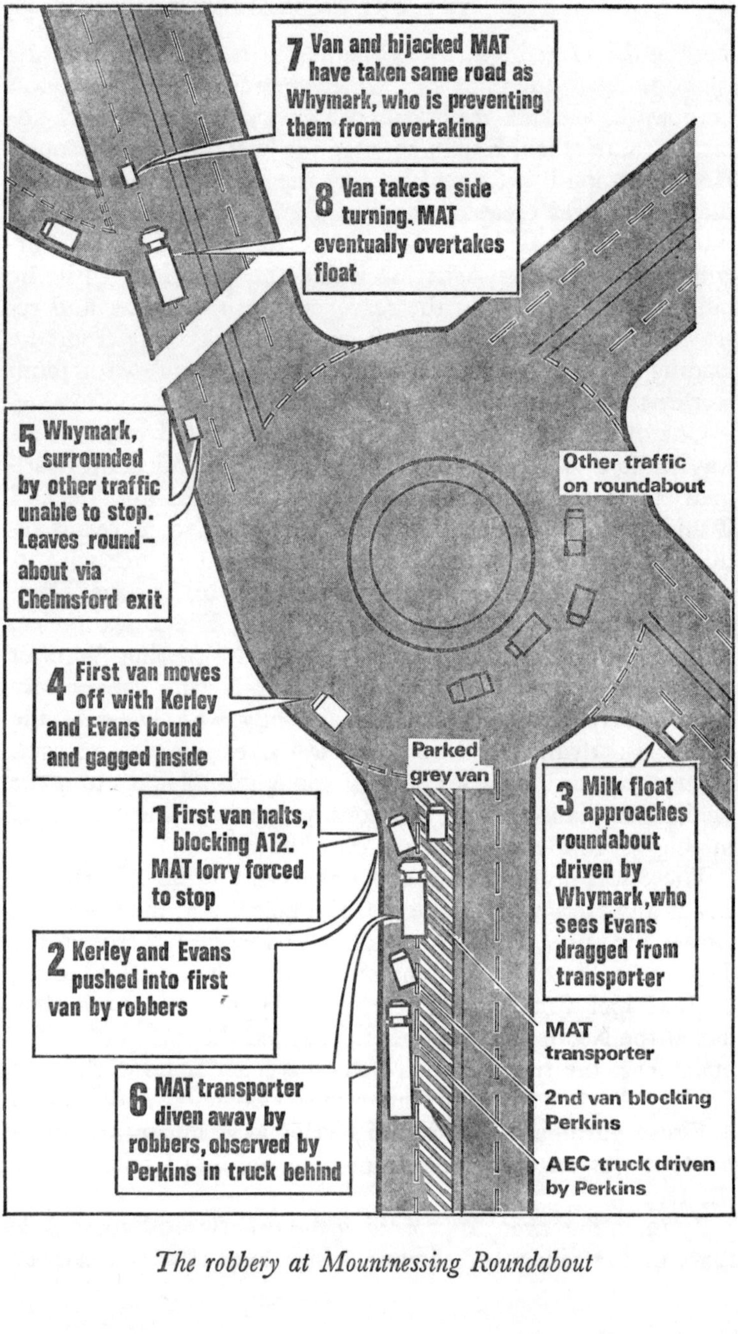

The robbery at Mountnessing Roundabout

through which the A12 passes. Nowadays there is an underpass and A12 traffic rushes under the roundabout. But on May 2, 1972 the underpass was still being built, so the roundabout was unavoidable. The A12 was painted with yellow 'slowing down' stripes as it entered the roundabout, and as they approached it Evans and Kerley noticed that there was a grey van parked in the offside lane.

The MAT lorry had just overtaken an eight-wheeler AEC truck driven by Raymond Perkins, a driver for a firm of clinker contractors. He was able to see much of what followed. The description of the robbery is based on the accounts of four people who saw it – Evans, Kerley, Perkins and the driver of a milk float who came on to the scene a few moments later. Perkins had just noticed the stationary grey van in the offside lane when a convoy of vehicles roared up behind him. A van overtook, followed by the MAT articulated truck, and then another large blue van which annoyed Perkins intensely because it cut in front of him to avoid hitting the stationary van and forced him to brake hard. The first of the vans to overtake Perkins drew into the nearside lane and stopped beside the stationary van in the offside lane. The way on to the roundabout was blocked, and Evans had to pull up.

From that moment everything happened very rapidly. One man who had been standing on the verge opposite the original stationary grey van ran up to Kerley's side of the cab. He was wearing a blue boiler suit and there was another man with him. Both appeared to be carrying iron bars or some similar weapon. They told Kerley to get out. His door was locked. He unlocked it, grabbed his coat and his bag, and clambered down from the cab. He was pushed into the back of the van which had just overtaken and finally blocked off the dual carriage way.

Another two men went up to Evans' side of the cab. One, he thought, was brandishing a small gun. Evans remembers him saying: 'Get out or I'll shoot.' Evans opened his door and began to get out. He was roughly pulled out and shoved into the back of the same van as Kerley. The roller shutter was dropped. There were other men in the back of the van. Kerley and Evans both had chain wound around their ankles and wrists and balaclava helmets pulled over their heads. Sticking tape was wound around the helmets and cotton wool was pushed under the helmets and into their ears. Kerley complained that he couldn't breathe, and some cotton wool was taken out of the helmet. He could hear a little conversation, and he could hear the crackle of a transistor radio tuned in to the police wavelength. The van moved off.

At the same time as all this was happening a milk float was driving slowly on to the roundabout. It was driven by Owen Whymark and it had come from the Brentwood direction. As he entered the roundabout he noticed the concentration of vehicles on the entry point from London and he realized something unusual was taking place. He could see Evans being dragged out of the cab, but he couldn't stop because there was other traffic around him on the roundabout. He took the Chelmsford exit.

As soon as the two MAT men had been removed from the cab one of the robbers clambered inside and the transporter moved off. Perkins, who had been forced to stop his truck behind the pile-up, noticed that the lorry was moving jerkily, as though the clutch was not being operated properly. The driver was obviously inexperienced in handling such a vehicle.

Whymark was driving his electric milk float slowly up the hill towards Chelmsford and was about a quarter of a mile out of the roundabout when he noticed that one of the vans he had seen on the roundabout was behind him. The engine was screaming and the driver was crashing his gears. The MAT lorry was behind it. Both vehicles were trying to overtake, but Whymark moved his float into the middle of the road and as there was traffic coming in the opposite direction he prevented them overtaking. Suddenly the blue van was no longer behind him; it had taken a turn-off. But right up behind the float and trying to overtake was the MAT articulated transporter with its load of bullion. It managed to get past and away, but Whymark read the number plate and jotted down the registration number on the back of a Giro cheque he had with him in the float. He drove on into the village of Mountnessing and within five minutes had pulled up outside the police house there. He described what he had seen to the policeman on duty and gave him the registration number. The alarm was raised, and police converged on the area from all directions.

Meanwhile the robber driving the MAT truck had turned left off the Chelmsford Road into Toby Lane. A short drive down narrow lanes brought him into the village of Swallows Cross, where a place called Chivers Farm was to be used for the unloading of the bullion. It was less than two and a half miles from the Mountnessing roundabout.

The van in which Kerley and Evans were bound and imprisoned was also taken to the farm. Other men were waiting there to transfer the bullion into a furniture lorry. Kerley was still inside the van when he thought he heard the noise of a fork-lift truck or some form of hydraulic lifting gear. The radio was on all the time the unloading of the bullion was being carried out, still tuned to the police VHF frequency, and that was how the robbers heard the alarm raised.

In many ways it was a well-planned crime. Clearly there was inside information about the nature of the load and the time the transporter would be passing through the Mountnessing roundabout. There were several men involved – just how many is still not known, but it seems there were at least eight. The locations for the hijacking and unloading, and the disposal of 643 silver ingots, all these were carefully pre-arranged. But such a crime was bound to involve risks. The most serious was that it was being carried out in broad daylight, in the middle of the day on a very busy road. The chances of there being no other traffic around at the time of the hijacking were almost non-existent, but presumably the organizers took that into account and still considered they would be able to get away with the robbery.

It all came down to timing: to the speed with which the actual hijacking was carried out and the transporter taken off the A12. The hijackers banked on having time enough at Chivers Farm to unload the twenty tons of silver and make their getaway before their crime could be detected. As there was no radio contact with the MAT offices and as the police were not keeping an eye on the vehicle no suspicions would be raised for a least a couple of hours, not until the transporter failed to arrive at Harwich, and if all went well then the hijackers, and the silver, would be miles from the area.

It might have worked but for Whymark, the milkman, slowing down the transporter when it was making its getaway, and reporting to the police so soon after the actual hijacking.

As soon as they knew from the radio that the police were searching for them the robbers decided to cut their losses and pull out of Chivers Farm. By this time they had transferred ninety-nine silver ingots, about £60,000 worth. The transporter was driven away and was later found abandoned in Wyatts Green Road, about a mile from the farm. It still contained more than 500 ingots. The furniture lorry into which some of the silver had been transferred was driven away. The van in which Kerley and Evans still lay bound and hooded was driven about a mile over bumpy roads to Doddinghurst and parked in a lane.

On the morning of the robbery Mrs Pauline Desmond went into Brentwood to do some shopping. When, at about 1.30, she returned to her home in Brook Lane, Doddinghurst, a narrow, unsurfaced road, she noticed a van parked on the right-hand side of the lane with a group of three men standing by it and another man standing on his own a little distance off. She stopped her car to take a look at the men, but as she did so they all turned away from her. She decided they must be gypsies and drove on to her house and began unloading the shopping. A little later she went outside the house again. The van was still there, but there was no sign of the men. Mrs Desmond became rather suspicious and went out to take a closer look.

After the van had come to a halt in Brook Lane and the engine had been switched off, Evans and Kerley heard the roller shutter being lifted and the men who had travelled with them getting out. The shutter came down again and Evans thought he heard a padlock being put on it. The two MAT men were still bound and blindfolded, but Kerley managed to work his hands free and took Evans' hood off and his own. They could now be sure they were alone, and they lit cigarettes, relieved that their ordeal had ended. They assumed they would not be able to get out of the rear door, so they decided to try to break down the partition separating the back of the van from the cab. They kicked at it and pulled it and eventually broke through, only to find that that there was a second partition beyond it. This too they broke down, and Evans clambered out of the van. Kerley hadn't been able to get out of the chains which bound his ankles. He stayed inside a little longer. Evans' wrists were still chained, but he could walk.

Mrs Desmond saw Evans and telephoned the police. Evans managed to get Kerley out of the van and to carry him towards Mrs Desmond's house. A short time later a car arrived from Ongar police station, driven by Police Constable Brian Ladd, who left two other officers to interview Mrs Desmond and drove off with another constable, Alan Kent. Their job was to comb the area, searching for any sign of the robbers who, it was assumed, must still have been in the area.

At about 3 pm the two constables were driving out of the village of Pilgrims Hatch along Ongar Road when suddenly, to the right, they noticed four men coming across a field from the Doddinghurst direction. It seems likely that these were the same four men Mrs Desmond had seen earlier in Brook Lane. Kent and Ladd noticed that they looked dishevelled and untidy, and they seemed to be labouring as though they had run a long way. Ladd stopped the car and leapt out. The four men spotted him, appeared to realize he was a policeman, and turned round and ran off in the direction from which they had come. Ladd immediately returned to the car to radio for help, while Kent jumped through the hedge and gave chase. One of the four men broke off from the others and ran in a different direction. Kent continued to chase the group of three men.

They crossed the field and went through a hedge on the far side. There was a patch of mud on the other side of the hedge and one of the men slipped and fell. He scrambled to his feet but by now Kent was close behind him. The mud was deep and the fleeing robber was up to his ankles in it when Kent grabbed him. He put up little resistance and Kent quickly snapped on the handcuffs. 'You're being arrested for a hijacking,' he said. 'Fair enough,' was the captured man's only reply. Kent asked him where the guns were. He said there were no guns. He refused to give his name and said he came from West Ham in London. Kent led him back towards the police car and by this time another car had arrived with reinforcements. The arrested man was taken to Brentwood police station. He was the only one caught in the hunt which immediately followed the hijacking.

Not far from the point where Kent made his arrest another policeman, Constable Anthony Collinson, was searching around an orchard at the end of Ash Close in Pilgrims Hatch. He had a police tracker dog called Blue with him. He had already looked round a farm next to the orchard and had found nothing. Suddenly he saw two men walking towards him across the orchard. When they saw him they changed direction but kept walking. Collinson went up to them. 'Where've you come from?' he asked. 'We've been walking over the fields,' replied one of the men. The other man had walked ahead, into the cul-de-sac end of Ash Close. Collinson shouted at him to stop, but he kept walking without looking back. The policeman grabbed hold of the first man and tried to catch up with the one walking ahead. The three of them, with the dog Blue, made their way down Ash Close towards its junction with Orchard Lane.

Also in Ash Close at the time was Mrs Ivy Asker, a housewife, who had spent the early afternoon of May 2 playing tennis at a local club. She had parked her car in Orchard Lane. After her game she had returned to the car, backed into the Close to turn round and was about to move off when she heard a noise behind her and turned to see a man approaching. Before she knew what was happening he opened the driver's door, grabbed her by the right wrist, and shouted, 'Get over.' He pushed her across the bench seat to the passenger side and revved the engine hard as he tried to engage gear.

A little earlier, Mrs Asker had been asked by a policeman if she had seen anything unusual in the area, so she realized something was up. She was frightened; she thought she was being taken hostage. She decided the only thing to do was get out, so she opened the passenger door and jumped out. As she did this Collinson, his dog, and the other man ran towards the car. The second man pushed Collinson to one side and leapt into the car beside the driver. Collinson tried to set Blue on to the man as he got into the car, but it was too late. The Hillman accelerated away at high speed into Orchard Lane.

The man PC Kent had arrested was taken to Brentwood police station, and soon after his arrival he was questioned by Detective Sergeant Donald Knight. Detective Constable Sidney Varey was also in the room when the interview took place. The man under arrest was frightened and angry. He was angry because he had been caught red-handed; not at the scene of the crime, not holding a bar of silver, but close enough to the robbery, soon enough after it, and in such suspicious circumstances that he knew there was no chance he was going to talk his way out of it. But most of all he was frightened. He did not know whether anyone else had been caught, and it was possible that he might be the only one questioned by the police about the planning of the crime, and worse, who else took part in it. The cardinal sin in the criminal world is to shop your partners, but the man knew that, alone with the police, the pressure on him to do so would be enormous. He did not look forward to his interrogation.

Knight did all the questioning, Varey sitting quietly beside him. The man had refused to give Kent his name, so that was the first matter Knight wanted to get out of the way. At first the man gave a false name and address, but it wasn't long before Knight got to the truth. The man apologized; he said the false name, John McGillan, was one he sometimes used, but he had made up the address. His real name was Anthony Sillett, and he lived in Alloa Road, Goodmayes. It was the same Golly Sillett the two women detectives had been watching earlier that day.

Sillett was full of excuses. He wasn't on the job himself, he said, he was only a loader. He had been dropped off in the country somewhere, and all he had to do was transfer some silver from one van to another. Then Knight asked the crucial question: 'Who else was with you?'

'There were about seven or eight of us altogether on the job,' Sillett replied. 'Look, they'll cut my throat if I tell you anything. I am as good as dead if I say anything.'

The interview was adjourned and continued later that afternoon. Sillett was nervous and pleading, asking the police if they couldn't do something for him. He knew nothing about guns, he said. All he knew was that he had been offered £2000 if he helped to unload the silver. The interview went on:

Sillett: Look, if I help you will you do something for me? I don't want to go down on my own for this. Haven't you got the others yet? You are bound to get them aren't you?

Knight: They must be out of the area by now.

Sillett: Look, I have got four kids and my house on a mortgage. Can't you help me, I am well in it? There must be something you can do for me if I tell you, but they will kill me if they find out I grassed.

But it was clear Sillett was going to name names; Knight had only to keep him talking and they would come out. Sillett, in no bargaining position, was trying to make some kind of deal before he actually told Knight any names. It is not unknown for the police to 'help' in the sense of pressing less serious charges, or recommending a lighter sentence at the trial, if the arrested man helps in tracking down others who have taken part in the crime. It is a sordid business: the criminal, alone with the police, starts weighing up his earlier friendships or criminal relationships against trying to make deals with the police to reduce the length of the inevitable prison sentence.

Sillett: I have been out of work for about three months and it looked like a godsend, so I took a chance on it. What a bloody fool I have been. I'll tell you the blokes I know but I won't put them in a statement or anything because I'm not kidding they will cut my throat. . . . I'm worried about my wife and kids in case they have a go. She doesn't know anything about this. I can see I'll get years for this.

Knight: This is the sort of thing you should have thought about before you started out.

And then Sillett gave the names of seven other people he claimed had also taken part in the hijacking. He gave the proper names of four of them. For the three others he gave only nicknames, and no surnames. Knight said he was not satisfied with the nicknames. He thought these were the men Sillett was frightened of and that was why he was holding back their real names. Only three of the men Sillett listed can be named here, the three who have been convicted of taking part in the Mountnessing bullion robbery. They were Frankie Sims, Ronnie Molloy and George Ince.

Sillett then made a statement from which the names were excluded, as agreed. He said:

> I have been working up to about three months ago, but I fell out with the chap I had been working with. Things have been a bit tight so when this job was put to me by a fellow I knew in a pub I thought I'd take a chance. He said if I did I would get a couple of grand. Later he told me there was this lorry of silver they were going to have over. I met this fellow several times before the job but it wasn't until last night that I knew it was going to be pulled today. I met this fellow this morning and we drove from his house round the corner where we picked up a van. There was another three men with the van. I sat in the back of the van, it was a big grey one, and we came down to Brentwood. They were going to hold up the lorry with the silver but they didn't say where. I was told that I had to unload the lorry after they had snatched it. From what I was told there was about eight of us on the job. They had some bars but on my life I never knew anything about guns. I would not have anything to do with that. I was dropped off at a place in the country about half-past eleven. There was a fellow already there. I just called him Mack, which was what the others called him. He had a big lorry. It was blue and black and roofed over. I had never seen him before. The others went off again. I just sat about. Later on they came back. They had the nicked lorry and then the van came back. As soon as the lorry pulled up Mack opened it up and we started to unload the silver into the other lorry. There was three of us unloading at first but two others came out of the van to help. One of the blokes said they had been seen and there was panic on. We just shifted some of the stuff when someone said, 'Get the lorry out.' I got in the van and saw the two blokes chained up in the back. The lorry went first but four of us went

in the van. We drove for about twenty minutes and then dumped it in this unmade road. One of the blokes who was tied up a bit too tight got one of the blokes to loosen him a bit. The four of us walked off across the fields then when we had been going some time a copper caught me. It seemed ages that we walked through woods and swampy ground before I was caught. The other three got away. On my life I didn't know any guns were going to be used. Honestly it was only that I wanted a few quid or I wouldn't have done it. I've told you all that I can. I wish I had never got involved.

Sillett was charged. And later he was found guilty of conspiracy to rob and sentenced to ten years in prison.

3 - East End childhood

GEORGE HENRY INCE was born on June 30, 1937, in a small terraced house in Bow, in the East End. The street, Robert's Road, had nothing to distinguish it from many similar ones in the area; the Ince family house was No. 4. It was hit badly during the blitz and no longer exists; nor does the road. George was the seventh child of James and Minnie Ince, who both came of old established cockney stock. James Ince worked, as his father had done, for the cleansing department of Stepney Borough Council, although it wasn't called that in his father's day. Both were dustcart drivers.

James Ince was orthodox, even perhaps a little strict, at home. Although his was a large family he would not consider Minnie going out to work. 'If you're married your place is indoors,' he used to say. At the time that George was born the family existed on the meagre weekly income of £2 7*s*, but the oldest child, Albert, was just about to start work and his contribution more than offset the extra mouth that had to be fed. The other children then were Rose, Margaret, Johnny, Phyllis and Betty. Another daughter, Pauline, was born later.

It was a very close family and the war split it up for the first time. Albert had a job as a van boy; Rose had left school and was looking for a job; the rest, except for George, were evacuated. On some occasions only James and Minnie, Rose and George were left at home. There was one such night in August 1940. James was on air-raid warden duty in Robert's Road. As the sirens started to wail he called in at No. 4. 'I think it's going to be a bad night,' he told Minnie. 'We'd be better off in the big shelter at the top of the road.'

As he spoke the bombs started falling. One hit the Lord Napier pub further up the street and killed the landlord. The Inces hurriedly gathered up a couple of pillows and blankets and prepared to move out, all except George, who had a reputation, even at the tender age of three, for being able to sleep through the heaviest raid. He rarely woke up even when carried to the comparative safety of the Anderson shelter at the bottom of the tiny garden. That night he was asleep in the downstairs room and when Rose told him to get up he refused to budge. He poured his customary scorn on the general alarm. 'Let them come, I'm not moving for that bastard Hitler,' he declared, or so Ince family legend has it.

It was his father who eventually picked him up and carried him up the road to the communal shelter. After a long, noisy night, the bleary-eyed residents of Robert's Road emerged at first light to find one whole side of the street practically demolished. No. 4 had been on that side. From the wreckage James and Minnie constructed a shelter; blankets were put up for walls. They lived like that for a couple of months before James managed to find another small terraced house for rent in Ireton Street, just behind the main Bow Road. It was to be the Ince family home for the next twenty-seven years.

For a brief period at the end of 1940 the whole family was together again. Then Albert went into the army and Phyllis, Betty and George were evacuated to Stourbridge in Worcestershire. They were not at all keen on the idea; they liked London in spite of the bombs. Before the devastating raids on dockland in the late summer of 1940 East Enders had gained a reputation for being reluctant evacuees; mothers refused to surrender their children even after special house-to-house canvasses by the Home Office. The concerned local newspaper, the *Stratford Express*, ran a campaign to comfort worried mothers separated from their children, getting teachers who had gone with the first evacuees to send in reports saying how nice it was in the countryside or how much the children were enjoying the hot summer and trips to the seaside.

When the first sirens started their eerie whine they were greeted with the same stubbornness. One of the first warnings was at a Sunday lunchtime. The *Express* reported there was 'annoyance concerning the time at which Hitler had caused them to be sounded . . . some stayed at the dining table and proceeded to get on with the roast beef and Yorkshire pudding'.

Phyllis, Betty and George spent the first two days of their evacuation in a Stourbridge school. This was the loneliest time for evacuees, when they were particularly prone to homesickness: everything was rushed and allotting places in families took time. Wherever possible, brothers and sisters were kept together, but they couldn't house all three Inces under one roof; they found room for George and Betty with a Mrs Maley and Phyllis was put in the house opposite. During the long wait in the school hall the trio decided to run away back to London. The plan was to meet after they had had their tea.

Betty, who was ten at the time, was the expedition leader. She told Mrs Maley they were just going to collect Phyllis and go for a walk up the road. Mrs Maley thought that would be all right as long as they did not stay out too long. Betty agreed and led George by the hand out of the house. They knocked on the door opposite and Phyllis joined them. Without having the slightest notion about directions, they set off to walk back to London.

Betty had a vague thought that if they could reach the railway line the simplest thing to do would be to walk along it. But they never found it. It got dark and cold; George was very tired and wanted to go to bed. They came to the outskirts of a town and Betty stopped a woman.

'We're lost,' she said.

'Where have you come from?' asked the woman, alarmed to find three small children wandering about aimlessly in the middle of the night.

'Stourbridge,' said Betty, proudly.

'That's impossible,' said the woman, 'this is Birmingham. Your home is twelve miles away. How did you get here?'

'Walked,' said Betty. 'We're on our way to London.'

An air-raid warden joined the little group and offered to take the kids home and give them a cup of tea, but the woman insisted that the police should be called. 'So, we spent the night in the nick,' Betty recalls. 'In the morning we explained to the police, who were very nice, that we wanted to go back to London, but they took us to Stourbridge and everyone made a great fuss of us there.'

And there they stayed for the next two years. James and Minnie visited them as often as possible and they were happy enough. George in particular grew to like the country and developed a special affection for Mrs Maley's boxer dog.

By the middle of 1944 the Ince family was reunited in No. 27 Ireton Street, except for Albert, who was still in the army. It was the era of the V2s. George was developing into a wiry youth and was learning how to stick up for himself in the rugged existence forced on East Enders by the concentrated bombing. But there were two serious setbacks from which he very nearly did not recover. The first was a simple home accident. He was swinging on a cupboard door in the scullery of No. 27 Ireton Street while his mother was cooking up a stew. Suddenly he slipped and grabbed at the handle of the stewpot, bringing the boiling mixture down on top of him. It covered his whole body. Minnie, following advice from an old wives' tale, poured flour all over him, bundled him into a pram and rushed him round to St Andrew's Hospital. It was touch and go for several days and he still bears the scars. Not long after this incident he had a severe bout of pneumonia and spent a further period in hospital.

The whole family helped to nurse George back to health. Back at school he got involved in street scraps as much as the rest of them, and being a small child he sometimes had to adopt slightly unconventional methods of defence: if he couldn't reach them with his fists he used a cricket bat – with great success on one particular occasion, his sisters remember. It was during this period that George came to terms with the realities of East End life. The families who lived in the tiny hamlets which grew up east of the Tower of London had developed intense loyalties, and the children learned, often from painful experience, that accounts were settled within the resources of the family – outside help was never called upon. If it was a personal score, then it was settled personally.

James and Minnie had a rule about this: if any of the children came home crying after a brawl they were told to 'get back there and give as good as you got'. If they didn't then they got a good hiding. Revenge was often a family affair. If George got the wrong end of a scrap, Betty and Phyllis would wait on a selected victim. Similarly, if the girls came home complaining of remarks being passed at them by a certain boy, George would settle the score sooner or later. That way nobody got the better of them.

The high spot of the year for the children, and their only break from Ireton Street, was the hop-picking. As East End families had done for generations, all the Inces except for the father moved down to Kent for the month of September. They had three small, oil-lit wooden huts on a farm, two used for sleeping and the other for eating. Minnie prepared the meals on ex-war department field kitchens. They slept on straw palliasses, sometimes four or five together, but like all the families were deeply house-proud: the fragile plywood walls of the huts would always be papered during the season, and when they could afford it they painted the walls to cover up the cracks.

One social historian observed at the beginning of the century that hop-picking was 'an amusement with profit', but there was no profit in it for Minnie Ince, and she had to have the meagre seven or eight pence a bushel for the hops supplemented by part of James's wages from Bow. The girls took the picking very seriously, but it was rare to find either Johnny or George 'on the bin' before 11 o'clock in the morning – and that was after insisting on tea and toast in bed before getting up. In the afternoon they would disappear fishing, or trapping rabbits.

When George left school at fifteen he had no qualifications. He worked on building sites as a labourer and then as an asphalter. For a short spell he had a flower stall outside Wanstead railway station. He was always known as the quiet one of the family – some attributed it to shyness – and he hated any form of exhibitionism. He was an emotional boy who had a great love for animals: at one stage at Ireton Street there were ducks, chickens, budgerigars, tropical fish and a boxer dog, all belonging to George. But his character, like his father's, included a streak of puritanism: he complained if his sisters wore too much make-up and they had to watch themselves at parties. 'You'd know by the expression on his face if he didn't approve of the way you behaved,' one of his sisters remembers. She called it being protective when George became annoyed if boys made passes at them.

George was growing up in a part of East London which was witnessing the beginning of the era of the Kray twins, Ronnie and Reggie. They were dishonourably discharged from National Service in the army in the spring of 1954 but even at that stage Private Ronald Kray, late of the Royal Fusiliers, was known throughout Bethnal Green and Mile End as 'the Colonel'. Many youths in the area were easily impressed by their style, from Ronnie's Chicago gangster double-breasted suits to the efficiency with which he and his brother took over the run-down billiard hall in the dilapidated Regal Cinema in Eric Street, Mile End. Before the twins moved in, the place was frequently wrecked and the green baize cloth ripped off the tables. The twins put an immediate stop to all this and turned the place into a profitable concern.

Few youngsters who lived nearby escaped the Krays' influence altogether; some became directly involved. Ireton Street was only five minutes' walk from the Regal and George Ince often visited the billiard hall and witnessed the twins' 'economic miracle'. But this contact did not become significant until several years later. Over a period of time he fell in love with the very attractive wife of the twins' elder brother, Charlie. She was always at Charlie Kray's side at the fabulous parties thrown by the twins. It was at one such party that George first met her, towards the end of the fifties. No open vendetta was waged against him for his effrontery in falling for her, but no one in the East End doubts that the two painful, violent incidents in which he later became involved, and which left him maimed for life, resulted from his affair with Dolly Kray.

The law was content to remain outside these East End confrontations, but did not turn a blind eye to some of George's other exploits. He first crossed the police's path in 1955, when he was seventeen. He was caught tampering with the locks of car doors in the Roman Road, found guilty of loitering and being a suspect person and put on probation for twelve months. The family was concerned, but not overmuch; kids were always being picked up for that sort of thing and there was no evidence of a deliberate criminal act, as far as they could see. In any case, George would soon be doing his National Service and that would keep him out of trouble.

Like many East End boys, including the Kray twins, he joined the Royal Fusiliers and was stationed at the Tower of London. He did not care for it at all. He had always been a loner and took a singular dislike to sharing his private life with others. For him, the army simply put greater restrictions on his freedom and offered him nothing in return – not even travel. But he never complained, at least not to his family. The only outward sign of his discontent that they noticed was his reluctance to return to barracks after a weekend at home. He was beginning to accept the idea of two years of unrelenting boredom when an opportunity came to cut it short. By this time Albert and Johnny were married; Betty and Phyllis had gone to work in Canada. After years of struggling to bring up their large family, James and Minnie had decided to separate. This left Minnie at home with George's youngest sister, Pauline, who was still at school. George put in a request for a discharge on compassionate grounds to look after his mother and sister. It was granted. He could hardly believe it, but within a few weeks he was back at home.

George took up asphalting again; it was a steady job. But just a month before his twentieth birthday he was involved in his first serious incident. He used to spend most evenings out of the house in Ireton Street meeting friends in Mile End, but for some reason, one of his sisters recalls, on that night in the summer of 1957 he had decided to stay in until about nine before going for a walk along the Mile End Road. Outside Bow police station he met some friends and they passed some 'unfortunate remarks' at two policemen in plain clothes who came out of the station. There was a scuffle. One of the officers was hurt. George was sent to prison for nine months for assault causing actual bodily harm. The family were badly shaken. At the court hearing none of them had thought that prison would result. His time was spent in Wormwood Scrubs and according to one of his sisters it changed his outlook on life; he became very impressed by the exploits of the 'more experienced' prisoners. A year after his release, in November 1958, he was involved in a café brawl with two men. He was given six months for causing grievous bodily harm: one man had been hit over the head with a bottle.

There were no other incidents for almost three years, but in the summer of 1961 he and a childhood friend broke into a radio and TV shop and took the £9 12*s* that was in the till. He skipped bail but was later sentenced to two years' corrective training for shop breaking and larceny. In view of his previous record it was a particularly harsh sentence. George was 'on the run' until 1963 when the police caught up with him. He served most of the sentence in Maidstone jail. But the family never forgot him and visited him regularly.

Out of prison again George plodded along as a builder, working more and more on his own. It left him plenty of spare time and he took up two popular East End pursuits: pigeon racing and the dogs. Outwardly he did not lead an exciting life and his friends tended to be much older than himself: he preferred it that way. He was particularly popular with the older members of the South West Ham Pigeon Club. His birds, kept in his sister Rose's back garden, won several minor prizes and, in 1966, one of pigeon racing's most coveted awards – the Berwick Trophy. The race is over the 304 miles from Berwick-on-Tweed in Scotland to London. His pigeon club colleagues remember him as a quiet, smartly-dressed young man, always ready to do someone a favour. George left the club in 1968 when Rose had to move out of her home because it was being demolished under a local authority housing scheme. He had nowhere to keep his birds as by that time he had moved into his skyscraper council flat in Hathaway Crescent, Manor Park.

It was from this period that George began to see more of Dolly Kray, visiting her regularly at her council flat in Poplar (Charlie and the Kray twins had been in custody since May 1968). There were always a number of people around who were anxious to make a name for themselves, and physically assulting someone who had crossed the Krays was an easy way of going about it. But the family's warnings were tempered with understanding: they knew how fond of Dolly George was; it was impossible to advise him to stop seeing her.

The first physical attack was in 1969. Three men burst into George's flat and shot him in the leg. They then systematically broke every bone in the fingers of both his hands. He was operated on and the smashed bones were replaced with steel pins. George's explanation of his condition to the hospital staff – and to the police – was that he had been involved in a family row.

The second attack came two years later in 1971. He was hit on the head as he left his flat, bundled into a car, and, in classic style, taken for a ride. Two men held him down in the back of the car, while another pushed a shotgun down his trousers and pulled the trigger, clearly aiming at his genitals. But George was struggling and the blast hit his leg, blowing off part of the calf muscle instead. He was dumped outside Middlesex Hospital where ninety-three lead pellets were later removed from his leg. Another thirty-five are still there. That time he told the police he had been involved in a hunting accident.

In a third attack the following year, he was shot while getting into his car after he had come out of a pub in the East End. The bullet went wide of its mark. George never revealed the identity of any of his attackers and one can safely say that he never will. He has always stuck rigidly to the 'no narking' conventions of the East End. In the meantime his family are always afraid that his attackers will continue to abuse the freedom from prosecution that this code allows them.

His family was also aware that his association with Dolly Kray was not the only problem. He had been in the company of friends of the Tibbses, a large and well-known family of East End scrap-metal merchants. Because of a family feud, the Tibbses had their enemies, and George's friendship with them meant that their enemies were also his. When members of the Tibbs family and their associates were arrested by Scotland Yard's 'gang-busters' in the spring of 1972, George reckoned that sooner or later he would be arrested or, at best, called to give evidence. That of course he could never do, and it was for this reason, he later told a court, that at the end of April 1972 he left his flat in Manor Park.

On May 21 three men booked into the Endcliffe Hotel, Margate, on the seafront. They said they would like to stay for an indefinite period; they were working on generators at Manston airport. They did not sign the hotel register, which was nothing unusual; hardly any of the guests did. They gave their names as George Ince, Ronald Molloy and Frank Sims. They were a sociable trio, mixing easily with the other guests, although Ince tended to be a little on the quiet side. They left for the Bank holiday, but came back afterwards and stayed until the beginning of August. They spent a lot of time on the beach and Ince got very suntanned: he was jokingly referred to by the hotel staff as an illegal immigrant.

4 · The murder hunt

'*The major question in this case is one of identity. Evidence of identification always presents many hazards.*' – Mr Justice Melford Stevenson, summing up in the first Barn murder trial of George Ince.

AT precisely 2.32 am on Sunday November 5, 1972, a telephone operator on the Braintree exchange took an emergency call from Braintree 656. He recognized the number immediately as the Barn restaurant. The exchange, which had not been converted to STD, often received calls around this time from the Barn for taxis for homeward-bound diners. The caller was David Patience, and his voice was anxious: he said that his father had just told him that there had been a robbery and someone had been shot. The call was transferred immediately to Braintree police: the Barn murder investigation had begun.

Sergeant Maurice Vowles and PC Hasler, from Braintree police station, were the first to arrive at the Barn, less than fifteen minutes after the emergency call had been made. Vowles was met at the door of the Sun Lido House by Bob Patience in evening dress. He had a crudely knotted tie hanging round his neck as though someone had tried to strangle him. His face was covered in blood from a wound behind his right ear. 'For God's sake get them to hospital,' yelled Patience, pointing at his wife and daughter lying on the floor in the front room.

Mrs Patience was having difficulty in breathing and there was blood on her face. Vowles turned her over on her side to prevent her choking. Beverley was on her stomach. She was complaining of a pain in her back, but Vowles could not immediately see any wound. She was conscious, but kept saying she couldn't breathe. She had a pair of nylon tights knotted round her neck. The ambulance arrived and as Mrs Patience was being lifted on to a stretcher Vowles found the first important clue, a small-calibre cartridge case which fell out of her clothing on to the carpet. He put it on a table with another one he found near Mrs Patience. Patience got into the ambulance with his wife and daughter and as it pulled away across the gravel forecourt of the restaurant another police car arrived, with Detective Chief Inspector Wyatt.

The shooting had happened on Wyatt's 'manor', as he likes to call it: he was chief CID officer in the part of Essex that included Braintree. At 3.15 am he walked into the Sun Lido House and took charge of the inquiries. There were two lines to follow immediately: the raiders had made their getaway in David Patience's blue Volkswagen estate car: a description of the car was radioed to all local police controls. Secondly, the diners and dancers who had been at the Barn that night had to be traced and interviewed. The appointments book was checked. Wyatt set the inquiries going and left for Black Notley Hospital, about two miles away, where the Patiences had been taken.

As Beverley was being transferred from the ambulance to one of the hospital stretchers, the ambulance driver loosened her blouse and a bullet which had gone right through her body fell out on to the floor of the casualty department. Nurses cut away her blouse and bra but she was still having trouble with her breathing. They gave her oxygen before taking her away for an X-ray. She was later transferred to the intensive care unit.

An X-ray of Mrs Patience's skull showed that a bullet was firmly embedded in her brain. It had entered just above her right eye and brain matter was oozing from the wound. After hurried consultation it was decided that she should be transferred to the neurosurgical unit at Oldchurch Hospital, Romford, thirty miles away. Bob Patience's ear was cleaned and a dressing applied; an X-ray revealed no damage and he was put in a recovery ward for security reasons. When Wyatt arrived he had a brief talk with Patience and then ordered that all three should have armed guards by their bedsides.

*   *   *

The first major break on the inquiry came as Beverley was being prepared for an emergency operation. A farmworker, Arthur Goult, was driving a tractor along the main A120 towards Braintree at about 8.15 am when he saw a car abandoned in a field by the roadside. It was David Patience's blue Volkswagen. The fingerprint experts set to work on it, but found nothing which would be of any help.

Meanwhile David Patience was checking to see how much had been taken from the safe. He discovered that cash and cheques had been stolen. The police interviewed him in the Cavalier Bar of the restaurant about four hours after his father, mother and sister had been taken to hospital. They asked him if he could describe the men he had seen driving his car away. He hadn't seen the driver at all and had only caught a glimpse of the passenger. He did not mention the colour of his eyes, nor of his hair; he had been up for twenty-four hours and was deeply shocked by what had happened. It wasn't until about a week later that he gave a description to the police. It was all verbal; nothing was written down. He recalls that he was shown a few photographs at different times and he saw, more by accident than design, some lying around the 'incidents room' (the centre for collating information) which the police had set up at the Barn. None of the photographs he saw was like the man he had seen that night in his car. The fact that the man's eyes were blue did not strike him until after he had seen, and read, the Photofit description in the papers.

During that Sunday the detectives busied themselves with setting up their inquiry headquarters in a room next to the Barn restaurant. In the course of trying to establish motives for the raid, they were studying files brought from London concerning the brawl outside Patience's old club the Ranch House in Ilford in 1961. They thought that there might be a connection.

The first police briefing to the press was early that afternoon: the attackers were described as 'so cold-bloodedly callous as to be on the verge of insanity'. Journalists learned of reports that Patience had been tipped off, at least a month previously, about a possible raid on the restaurant. Rumours about a robbery had been mentioned at Chelmsford Crown Court the Tuesday before the shooting, when David Patience had unsuccessfully appealed against fines totalling £100 and an eighteen-month driving ban for speeding and failing to stop for the police. Bob Patience told the court that he had warned his son to be careful because he had heard that a raid was planned on 'a certain restaurant' in Essex and he was sure it was the Barn. Though David Patience had pleaded guilty at the original hearing at Braintree Court on August 31, at the appeal he said he had thought the two police officers who tried to flash him down might have been robbers.

In fact the warning had come in May, in a phone-call from a publican friend to Majorca, where Patience was on holiday with his wife and Beverley. On his return to England he had been given police protection almost every night for about two months. When nothing happened, the protection was lifted. Importantly, the Majorca call was not the first indication that Patience's flourishing business was being singled out by thieves as a possible target. Almost exactly a year before the November 5 attack two local youths had broken into the Sun Lido House and stolen some jewellery. No one had been in the house. Patience knew the timing was significant: if they had tried to break into his house before the end of October it is more than likely that they would have been seen by the caravanners in the trailer park at the back of the motel. So the discovery of two more raiders a year later did not come as any great surprise.

Wyatt's first task was to compile descriptions of the two men. His remarkable interview with Beverley is recorded in the Prologue, but it was Bob Patience who compiled the first Photofit picture of the gunman. He made up the picture at the Black Notley under the supervision of Detective Sergeant Rampling from Harlow police station. (Photofits are compiled from photographs of faces cut into various sections. More than five hundred million variations can be compiled from the standard kit. The witness selects the features which, in his opinion, bear the closest resemblance to the person he is identifying.)

The nose, mouth and chin of Patience's picture of the gunman were amended by Beverley, and Patience agreed that it had been improved. A picture of the accomplice was then made up by Patience; Beverley again amended it, altering the chin slightly. Patience, who was continually amazed at the amount Beverley could remember, agreed that it was a better likeness.

Thus by the end of the second day the police were in possession of good descriptions of the two men, most of the detail having been provided by Beverley. The descriptions may be summarized as follows:

The gunman: Age: early thirties. Sandy blond hair, combed forward from the crown, short, no sideboards. About 5′ 8″ tall, slim build. Very blue eyes with a sallow complexion. Even white teeth with lips a little on the full side. He was wearing a beige/stony kind of mac and brown old-fashioned shoes with a kind of buckle on the side and chiselly toes. He spoke with a very slight Yorkshire accent and had said he came, as he had told Beverley and her mother, from the Yorkshire area.

The gunman's accomplice: Dark-haired. Aged about twenty-seven/eight, taller than the other – about 6′ 1″ or 2″, slim with broad shoulders and a slim waist. Dark hair parted at one side, with short sideboards. His hair was longer than the first man's and it flicked up a little at the back. He had brown eyes and a slim face.

Beverley thought one of them had a mole on one of his cheeks. It might have been the blond one, she wasn't sure. The dark one was wearing a light-grey tweed suit. He had a tartan-coloured scarf with beige and blue in it, and was carrying a black or brown briefcase. She was certain that both men had been wearing black leather gloves. If that was true Wyatt knew that it was most unlikely that he was going to find any fingerprints of the men; microscopic forensic evidence of this kind would be confined to the men's clothing. All that had been established by the forensic department so far was that the gun used had been a ·32 calibre weapon: two cartridge cases and two spent bullets that had been found confirmed this.

On November 7, the Tuesday after the shooting, the police saw their first 'volunteer witness' – that is, someone who had not been anywhere near the Barn on the night of the shooting. He was a disabled serviceman called Jonathan Ridley, who lives less than a mile from the Barn, just off the Rayne Road going towards Braintree. It was Ridley who had been asked the way to the swimming baths in Rayne Road by two strangers on the morning of Saturday November 4. Next day one of his neighbours came into his council flat, told him of the Barn shooting down the road, and that the police were looking for two men. Though he had thought nothing of it at the time, Ridley then remembered the odd encounter with the two men. Wouldn't it be a coincidence if these were the same men who had raided the Patiences' home?

Ridley's wife thought that he should go to the police and tell them, even if it turned out in the end that his information was of no use. At first he was reluctant. Apart from the fact that his information seemed to him to be of little more than passing interest the prospect of going down to the Braintree police station was not a pleasant one for him. His health was not good: he had been a prisoner-of-war with the Japanese in Singapore for three years, had also been part of the slave labour force which built the bridge on the River Kwai, and nowadays he got short of breath very quickly. But his wife insisted. At Braintree police station the sergeant on the desk thanked him for coming in and said that detectives would probably be in touch with him.

On the following Tuesday afternoon two detectives called at Ridley's home and showed him the Photofit impressions compiled by Beverley and her father in hospital. He found that the first one – that of the gunman – was very similar to the man he had seen. But he was uncertain about one particular feature: the mole below the right eye. In the tape-recorded descriptions on the day after the shootings Beverley had told Wyatt that one of the two men had a mole below his eye. She was not sure whether it was the gunman or his accomplice who had the mole, but it had now been put on the Photofit of the gunman. Ridley was unhappy about it: he remembered that there was something wrong with the man's eye. It looked like a cast or, as he described it, a 'lazy-type' eye. The Patiences' Photofit of the accomplice, he thought, was a very fair impression of the dark-haired man who had asked him the way to the swimming baths. He thought he would probably recognize the first man again, but was less certain about the accomplice.

The police were now presented with a major problem over the descriptions – whether they should include the mole below the right eye on the gunman's face or not. The mole was clearly of the utmost importance for it was an unmistakable feature. The police decided, again, to give it to the gunman. That same day they released the Photofit to the press, and it appeared in the national papers of November 8. (The second Photofit, although ready, was not released.) From the full description given to reporters by the police two prominent features were selected by the crime writers: the mole below the right eye and the man's northern accent.

All the papers mentioned the 'substantial' reward offered by Bob Patience for information leading to the arrest and conviction of the attackers. The sum was not disclosed. But behind the scenes Patience had agreed with the police to make it £1000; later, on their advice, he raised it to £2000.

When he left hospital on Wednesday morning, November 8, Patience had a bulky dressing stuck over his left ear, and was obviously suffering from the terrible strain of the past few days, but outwardly he was composed enough to speak to reporters and later to go on to TV. Before that he was taken to Oldchurch Hospital, Romford, to see his wife. He reached her bedside just three minutes before she died. On coming out of the hospital Patience issued a terse warning to the two raiders. 'My wife is now dead,' he said. 'If it takes all the money I have I will see justice done to these two fanatical and despicable men.'

The police followed up Patience's offer of money with an appeal to the 'underworld' for help in tracing the killer; names had already been pouring in from that source. Detective Chief Inspector Barry Tarbun told reporters: 'We are still making inquiries on the names that are coming up from the criminal fraternity.' The Essex CID chief, Detective Chief Superintendent Cecil Leonard White, who had assumed overall control of the whole inquiry, felt that the horror of the crime would cause someone to come forward with information. Sometime during that first week – the police have never said precisely when they received the crucial call – one anonymous caller mentioned George Henry Ince, a builder from East London.

It was a turning-point in the inquiry. Beverley's description of the gunman was close enough to Ince in major details for the police to act. They established that Ince had a criminal record for shopbreaking, larceny and assault, and available descriptions gave him light-brown hair, blue eyes and 5′ 10″. Wyatt, who had been showing Beverley and Bob Patience large numbers of photographs of men who could have fitted their recollections, narrowed the field immediately. On Friday November 10 he compiled a set of twelve photographs, numbered them from 1 to 12 and marked the set with the letter A. George Ince was put at No. 3.

The photograph Wyatt had selected was one which Ince had had taken for a passport in April 1971 – eighteen months before the Barn raid. The passport had been found in Ince's flat in Manor Park when the police had searched it on May 3, the day after the bullion hijacking. Ince had, characteristically, dressed immaculately for the photo. His hair was brushed tidily; he had a white shirt and spotted tie, neatly knotted up to the collar, and an expensive-looking jacket. It was a posed photograph; his body was slightly inclined to the camera. It was, it can fairly be said, a very different kind of photograph from the other eleven. They were all police pictures, with the full face to the camera. Eight of the men were wearing identifiable striped prison shirts; the other three were roughly dressed. At least two of them appeared to have dark brown hair; Beverley had described the gunman as blond as opposed to fair. Five of the men appeared solidly built; Beverley had described the gunman as definitely slim.

At about 5 pm Wyatt visited Beverley at Black Notley Hospital together with Len White. She had required, as the surgical registrar put it, very careful supervision since her emergency operation. She had developed a prolonged ileus – a complete absence of bowel activity – but a fluid diet was beginning to correct it. A large drain had been placed near the entrance to her stomach where it had been damaged by the bullet.

Wyatt recorded his meeting with her thus: 'After a considerable period of time in which she studied and eliminated various of the photographs she eventually indicated to me the photograph No. 3 – that of George Ince.' Wyatt then took the set of twelve into a small private office next to the intensive care unit and showed them to Bob Patience. He studied them and finally picked out photograph No. 6 on the top line and No. 8 on the bottom line as bearing the closest resemblance to the gunman.

It is not possible, for obvious reasons, to reproduce the card of twelve pictures. But it is important to try and estimate the value of Bob Patience's choice of Nos. 6 and 8. In the opinion of the authors No. 6 bore a much closer resemblance to Brook, particularly the eyes and high cheekbones, than the passport picture of Ince. No. 8 did not, in the authors' opinion, look like Brook.

Wyatt now had two positive lines to work on: the anonymous phone-call naming George Ince and the identification of Ince by Beverley. The following day, Saturday, he sent detectives to three addresses in East London: to Ince's sister, Rose Threadwell; to his lover, Mrs Grey, and to Bill Cannon, Ince's friend from his pigeon-racing days.

Rose Threadwell was living in a new house on a council estate at Manor Park, and working in the accounts department of the Watneys Brewery opposite the estate (coincidentally, the same brewery that supplied beer to the Barn restaurant). That afternoon she had been out shopping with her husband, Jim, and had left a key to the front door under the mat outside – something she had hardly ever done before, but she thought her son might get back before her. She came home shortly after 4 o'clock and a neighbour called out to her. The police had been, stayed some time, and apparently searched the house.

'What on earth did they want?' asked Rose.

'I don't know,' said her neighbour. 'They didn't say.'

Within a few minutes of the Threadwells' return the police had surrounded her house and were knocking at the door. Jim

Threadwell, a quiet serious-minded man in his mid-fifties, answered it.

'I'm Detective Inspector Johnson,' said the policeman. 'We've had a phone call that the two men wanted for the Barn restaurant murder are at this address. We were told we'd find the key under the mat.'

'I don't know what you're talking about,' said Jim, who could see several other policemen outside. In fact there were eight of them.

'Haven't you heard of that murder?'

'Oh, yes,'

'Well, has your brother been here today?'

'Which one?' interrupted Rose.

'George,' said Johnson.

'No, he hasn't. He hasn't been here for months,' said Rose.

The police searched the house again and asked if Rose had any pictures of George; she hadn't. They told Jim they were all 'tooled up' and they meant business, which he understood to mean that they were armed. The police found nothing, and left the house.

Next on the list was Mrs Grey. There are two versions of what took place in her Poplar flat. According to Detective Inspector Derek May of the Regional Crime Squad, Mrs Grey became incoherent, verging on the hysterical, when she realized that her two visitors were police officers. He says he told her they wanted to know the whereabouts of George Ince and that there were rumours that she knew him. Asked when she last saw Ince she replied: 'At least eight years ago when we were all young.' Asked if she had seen him since, she replied: 'No, I don't know where he is. I have had nothing to do with him. I have got enough troubles with being under the psychiatrist and going in and out of hospital for my nerves.' As soon as they mentioned the Barn incident she had left them standing on the doorstep while she made a telephone call. Then she had let them in. She told them that she had phoned a Mr MacArthur, her solicitor, who had told her to ring whenever the police came to see her. Before they left the flat the police asked Mrs Grey again if she had seen Ince and she replied: 'I don't know why people keep asking. I only knew him eight years ago.' That is how Inspector May recalled the meeting. He and another officer, Detective Sergeant Moore, searched the flat and stayed with Mrs Grey for about twenty minutes.

Mrs Grey's recollections are somewhat different. She says the policemen never mentioned the Barn murder. When she was asked about Ince she told them that she had known him for a number of years and that he used to go to the billiard hall in the Mile End owned by her brothers-in-law. She claims she never said anything about only having known him eight years ago; that she told the police that she had known him for fourteen or fifteen years, and that they did not ask if she had seen him recently.

The police investigation had reached a crucial stage. The phone-call they had received had been from someone who not only named Ince but knew him well enough to mention the two places where he was likely to be found on a Saturday afternoon or evening. It was quite on the cards that more information would be forthcoming from the same source. Ince had certainly seen both Rose and Mrs Grey on the evening of November 4, but he had not been in London at all during the following Saturday, November 11. He had spent the day in Kent and the night in his caravan in Whitstable. With Beverley's positive identification of him it was inevitable that the hunt would be stepped up.

But if the police were certain of their suspect the public were still to be kept guessing. Len White told reporters for the Sunday newspapers that a list of three hundred suspects had been built up and he believed the wanted men were amongst them. They would be caught, he forecast. An *Observer* reporter dug up an unusual angle: he reported that the police were working on a theory that the killers might have been army deserters. There were three points of circumstantial evidence. First, the cushion silencer was a technique frequently employed by the IRA. Secondly, the gunmen had short-back-and-sides haircuts which was 'nowadays rather unconventional for a man under thirty unless he was in the Services'. And thirdly,

Braintree was only fifteen miles from Colchester, which has a big army base.

On the Sunday after their first search for George in London, the police were contacted by a publican and his wife, Joseph and Ruth Ripton, from the Chequers Hotel, a red-brick Victorian pub in the village of Felsted, seven miles from the Barn. Their story was a curious one. They described how two men who could have fitted Beverley's descriptions of the gunman and his accomplice had been in the Chequers two days before the murder. Others in the bar confirmed the story, and the police had to investigate it. As it turned out it was irrelevant to the murder hunt, but it is included as a particularly interesting study of how a group of people attempt to recall the same event and to identify the same persons.

About 1.30 pm on Thursday November 2, they were serving in the bar of the Chequers when two men walked in and entered the private bar. Mrs Ripton was just going to tell them they were in the wrong part of the hotel when they left and came back again, this time into the public bar. One of them sat down and the other came up to the bar and ordered two brown ales and two rolls. Joseph Ripton recalled he was about six feet tall with neatly cut dark hair, small sideburns and wearing a short beige-coloured coat. The other man was shorter, about 5′ 9″, with shorter hair – almost a crew-cut. The hair was receding slightly. His wife agreed with the descriptions, but remarked that the second man had sandy or light-brown hair. The pub was quite busy at the time and she did not get a good look at them. The men sat together, not talking, for some time and then one of them left the bar for ten or fifteen minutes. At about 2.20 they both left and drove off in the direction of Braintree.

One of the regulars in the pub, a lorry-driver called Bunny Layzell, had taken particular notice of the two men. He had been in the public bar for several minutes before the two men came in, sitting on a stool at the bar and chatting to the Riptons. When Mrs Ripton told him that two men had tried to get into the private part of the house Layzell's curiosity was aroused. As the two men came into the public bar he took a long hard look at them. They were strangers to Felsted, that was definite: it was easy enough to pick out newcomers to the tiny village. But there was something else. Right from the start Layzell formed the impression, in his own words, that they were a right couple of bastards. It was their facial features that made him feel that way. They just looked like villains, he thought. And while they were in there during the next twenty minutes Layzell studied them with care.

The dark one, he noted, was slightly taller than the fair-haired one. His hair was not black, just a very dark brown, and he had a slightly fuller face than the other one. He was wearing a three-quarter length sheepskin jacket and a large gold signet-type ring on his finger. One of the most outstanding features of the fair-haired man was his protruding greyish-blue eyes. He was wearing a greyish-blue pinstripe suit with a matching waistcoat. When they left Layzell made a point of going to the window to see what kind of car they were driving. As it drew away he read out the number plate to Mrs Ripton. But later nobody could remember it.

While Layzell was watching the two strangers another man, Harry Leverett, who pays a weekly call to the pub to service the fruit-machine, came into the bar. His recollections of the two men were much the same as the others, but he was not as precise on details as Layzell had been: he did not recall any bulging eyes, nor could he remember their colour. The one thing that struck him as a little odd was that the men did not return his greeting when he entered the bar. Village people usually do, he had thought to himself.

The police thought the event might be significant. They saw Layzell and showed him the two Photofit pictures. Layzell thought that one of the Photofits fitted the fair-haired man exactly; the second was much the same as the second man, he thought. He had, however, seen the same picture in the papers a couple of days before. The day after they had been to see Layzell the police took the same Photofits to show Leverett and Joseph Ripton. Both agreed that the fair-haired man they had seen in the pub was similar to one of the Photofits: Ripton said the second man was also similar in appearance to the second Photofit. All three men, Layzell, Ripton and Leverett, were later to be witnesses on ID parades.

On the Sunday evening, one week after the murder, David Patience was in the sitting room of the Sun Lido House when he took a telephone call from a man who called himself Derek Davies. Davies said he had information about the robbery. He was not interested in the reward money but had just come out of prison, where he had heard people discussing robbing the Barn. He told David that the people came from the Braintree area and he could probably help to find them.

At this stage in the conversation David managed to get a policeman – they still had their incidents room set up next to the restaurant – to listen in to the call. Davies said he could call again the next day and tell David how he was going to arrive at Braintree so that the police could meet him. It was a dramatic moment, for this was a theory that the police had been working on – that the job had been hawked round by experienced thieves, probably in jails. The name Derek Davies meant nothing to David or to his father. Davies said the men concerned had mentioned that the best time to hit the Barn was bonfire-night weekend.

On the Monday night Davies called again at the pre-arranged time of 6 o'clock. This time the police monitored the call from the beginning. He again offered to come to Braintree but was not sure when he would be able to get the time off work, and in any case he did not have a car. David Patience said that he should hire one: the cost would be reimbursed. After the first call the police had moved very fast. By the time he rang again they had his picture; they showed it to David Patience, but he said it meant nothing to him. During the second call the police arranged a secret meeting with Davies. They had checked his background and thought his story quite credible.

The first the public heard about the new lead was in the morning papers on Wednesday. Reports mentioned the mystery caller who reckoned he knew the identity of the two raiders and said that he had asked for a round-the-clock armed guard because he was scared to death that he might be attacked for informing. Reports added that the police in fact already knew the names of two men they wanted to question but they 'had felt for some days' that at least four men were originally involved. They were still appealing to the public for anyone who had seen people acting strangely in the early hours of November 5. They received many calls and one of those they followed up concerned the strange affair of the mustard-coloured Volvo.

Ian Ransome, a student, told police that he had been driving home from Felsted towards Dunmow just after 2 am on November 5. When he passed through Little Dunmow he noticed a mustard-coloured Volvo 144 estate car parked without lights in the entrance to a junction called Bramble Lane off the main road. It was, thought Ransome, a strange place to be at that time of night. There was apparently just one man, the driver, inside.

A second witness was a customs officer at Stansted airport (only about ten miles from the Barn) called Raymond Hawkins. He was eventually to make a total of four statements to the police about what he had seen, the first of them on November 15, when he called the police after hearing that the getaway car used in the raid had been left in the immediate vicinity of a junction off the main A120 road to Felsted from Dunmow.

Hawkins had been called out at about 10 pm on the night of November 4 to investigate two people who had been found in possession of duty-free liquor at Stansted. He did not finish there until almost exactly 4.05 am when he got into his Morris 1100 to drive home to Felsted. He recalls the time when he left the airport because it takes him twenty to twenty-five minutes to complete the journey at night and he arrived home at exactly 4.30. The route he took was from Stansted to Takeley then on to Dunmow, where he turned left along the A120 to the Little Dunmow–Felsted turn-off. He passed several police cars on the way, one parked outside the Four Ashes pub at Takeley and three more at the Dunmow–Felsted turn-off.

Hawkins drove through the village of Little Dunmow, driving

very slowly because he was tired, and came to the Bramble Lane junction. On the grass verge on the far side of the turning he saw a car parked with its sidelights on. He thought the vehicle was moving out and was going to cross his path, even collide with him. He slowed down and put his lights on full beam and the vehicle seemed to stop. He then noticed that there was a second car on the opposite side of the junction, almost hidden from his view by a hedge, without lights. He saw someone walking between the two cars, but couldn't describe him, or tell in what direction he was walking. For a split second Hawkins thought he was going to be held up and robbed, but when the first car stopped he drove on. As he passed the car he saw two people in the front and a third in the back. Ten days after the event he described the person in the back as having long dark hair. The two in front, he thought, were men, but he was unable to describe them any further. He thought the car was British – a Cortina or an 1800, or something of that size, either fawn or cream, with plenty of chrome strip on it. The second car, which he could only just make out, he thought might have been a foreign car – possibly a VW Beetle. He had no idea if anyone was inside it.

The police came to the conclusion that it was quite possible that the student Ransome and the customs officer Hawkins had in fact seen the same car. Hawkins had seen an additional car which had arrived later on the scene. The whole scenario fitted well into the picture the police were building up of a total of four men taking part in the robbery. This isolated turning would have been an excellent place for the two who had actually carried out the robbery to be met by their colleagues for the final getaway. Ransome identified a police picture of a Volvo 144 estate car as the vehicle he had seen but made no more statements. Hawkins, on the other hand, was to make a further three. Taken in sequence they provide a fascinating study in retrospective identification. It must be remembered that when Hawkins first saw the two cars and the four men his own car had not come to a final halt. It was about 4.25 in the morning and still dark (although he had his headlights on full beam at the time), and he admits himself he was very tired, having been called out to the airport in the middle of the night.

Hawkins's three statements to the police, on November 19, 26 and 28, are reprinted in full below.

On November 19, Hawkins told Detective Constable Finch:

> Further to the statement I have already made I have now seen a car which I recognize as being very similar in style to the car I saw. This was a Triumph 2000 which has twin headlamps. I am therefore sure that the car I saw at the road junction with its lights on was a Triumph 2000.
>
> I am not able to help any further as to the other car other than it could have been a VW Beetle and it may have been a dark colour.
>
> I have thought about the people I saw in the Triumph 2000. The person in the front passenger seat was a well-built man with broad shoulders wearing a sports jacket or tweed suit. His hair was thick but not long with a parting towards the centre of his head and a wave falling on either side of the head. His face was round and full. I have been shown Photofits G7/72 and G7B/72 – these are in no way like the man I saw. I have also been shown Photofit G7A/72 and I feel if the chin was a bit higher and the line of the parting was a bit higher on the head and a bit more hair in a wave was on the shorter side of the hair, then this would clearly resemble the man I saw in the front seat of the car. The other features of this Photofit are correct.
>
> I have no recollection as to the other two people I saw in the car or of the person I saw in front.

On Sunday November 26, Hawkins was shown by Detective Constable Finch a number of photographs in an album marked 'B'.

> I looked at the eighteen photographs in an effort to identify the man I saw in the passenger's seat of the car I saw at 4.25 am on Sunday November 5, 1972. I cannot definitely identify any one of the people shown but I can say that the persons shown in photographs 3 and 10 bear the strongest resemblance to the man I saw. With both these photographs I feel I am being confused by the expressions on the faces. When I saw the man in the car I saw him with a look of astonishment on his face. The hair of the man No. 3 is too long down his neck but is otherwise

similar. The hair on the man No. 10 is not quite thick enough. The man No. 18 also bears some resemblance but his hair is nothing like as thick as that of the man I saw.

Two days later Hawkins told Detective Sergeant Murfitt:

> Further to my previous statements respecting sighting two vehicles and I believe four men, about 4.25 am on Sunday November 5, 1972, at the junction of Bramble Lane and the Little Dunmow/Felsted Road. On Tuesday November 28, 1972, I was shown one photograph of a man dressed in a white shirt and dark coloured tie, by the police. This man, I am fairly sure, was the man who was sitting in the front passenger seat of the car that was stationary across the Little Dunmow/Felsted Road.

Finally, on December 4, a month after he had first seen the two cars and the four men, Hawkins told Detective Constable Finch:

> I have previously made a statement about a car I saw at 4.25 pm on Sunday November 5, 1972. I have looked at a picture of a yellow-coloured Volvo 145 estate car and although from the picture I cannot be certain that this is the vehicle I saw, it certainly contains the features of the car that I saw with lights on and could well be the type of vehicle that I saw. I have previously referred to a Triumph 2000 but when I consider the front of these two vehicles they are very similar. The headlamp units appear to incorporate the side lights and again this is as I have already described. The amount of chrome at the front appears about right.

The same day that the police first saw Hawkins, November 15, they also interviewed Derek Davies, the mystery telephone informant. The meeting took place at a secret address. Harris was to say later that the information he had was of no help. But that information was not given to the Press that day. Len White said he was putting a stop on news releases 'because unauthorized information was being leaked'. He added that 700 statements from informants and witnesses had been taken and more than 1200 phone-calls received at the murder headquarters at the Barn.

The following day, November 16, the inquiry reverted to the Patience family. Beverley had had her stitches removed and had improved immensely. She was anxious to be released from hospital. But doctors warned that she had to have at least two months' rest to get over the shock of the shooting and her mother's death, and the police were anxious that she should not return home until the raiders were caught; it was suggested that she might go abroad until then.

November 16 was also the day the murder inquiry was mentioned for the first time in the House of Commons. Mark Carlisle, the then Minister of State at the Home Office, announced there would be an inquiry into David Patience's appeal against his speeding conviction. It had been requested by Arthur Lewis, the Labour MP for West Ham North, who told Carlisle that the shooting seemed to support David's explanation that there were grounds for believing that the men who were following his car were thieves, not police officers.

At the same time the search was hotting up for the sandy-haired, blue-eyed gunman whom the police described as a 'homicidal paranoid'. They had been to see Rose Threadwell again during the week and, according to her, had said that if he made a wrong move when they caught up with him, they wouldn't hesitate to shoot. They kept watch on the Threadwells' house, on Mrs Grey's flat and also on Ince's own flat in Manor Park.

On November 18, two weeks after the shooting, Wyatt and Harris went to see Beverley again in Black Notley Hospital. They again showed her the card of twelve photographs marked by the letter A, and she again picked out No. 3 – George Ince. Wyatt then showed her four more pictures of Ince and, finally, a fifth picture dated 1962. That picture had been given to Wyatt by the Criminal Records Office. It was taken after Ince had been arrested for stealing the £9 12*s*. from a TV shop in 1962. When Beverley saw the picture, she immediately sat upright in bed and, according to both Wyatt and Harris, looked very excited. She positively identified the man in the photograph as the one who had used the gun that night.

That Saturday evening the police waited for Ince to arrive either at Dolly Grey's flat or the Threadwells' house. He did, in fact, drive up to see Dolly, but he spotted the police outside the flat and returned to Whitstable immediately. His friends Sims and Matthews were surprised to see him. Usually when he went to London on a Saturday night he did not come back until the following morning. He met them in a pub in Whitstable. 'What are you doing back here?' they asked him.

'Well, it wasn't looking too good up there,' said George. 'To tell you the truth I nearly got my collar felt. They were all over the place.'

The police continued to focus their inquiries on Ince. Next day, November 19, they called again at Rose Threadwell's house. Her impression was that they were becoming very impatient. They warned her that they would arrest her for harbouring her brother if she was withholding any information about his whereabouts. And under no circumstances, they told her, should she continue to pay the rent on his council flat. But Rose Threadwell could tell the police nothing; she had not heard from Ince since the night of November 4.

The police thinking came out into the open for the first time in the London *Evening Standard* on November 20. No names were mentioned, but little room was left for doubt. The story ran:

> London's East End was being combed by police today for the gaunt, scarred gunman – a one-time associate of the Kray gang – who has been named by the Chief Constable of Essex as the killer of Mrs Muriel Patience. Named with him are four men, who may also have been involved in the November 5 shooting drama at the Barn Restaurant, Braintree, in which a gang escaped with £2000 after fatally wounding Mrs Patience. They also shot her husband and daughter.
>
> Essex CID chief, Detective Chief Superintendent Len White, who leads the hunt for the killer, said: 'No information regarding

anyone we are looking for has been officially released. I am not prepared to discuss any confidential message between police forces that we may have sent.'

But a team of Essex detectives, led by Mr White's deputy, Detective Superintendent George Harris, has been seeking the named man for more than a week. He has not had a permanent address for more than six months and efforts to find him have been abortive.

The man, who is well known in the East End and may have dyed his light-brown hair a sandy blond colour, was known at one time to have associated with the Kray twins.

The 35-year-old blue-eyed man being sought in the East End is described as having some old shotgun scars on his legs and a small scar on his left cheek. Police have been warned that he has a record of violence and may be armed.

He is five foot eight, gaunt and sallow with receding hair brushed forward from the crown. Identification of the killer and his accomplice may well eventually rely to a great extent on Beverley Patience, 20, who was shot in the back and was yesterday released from hospital . . .

The man was already being sought with four others in connection with inquiries into the theft of £60,000 worth of silver bullion – part of a £400,000 worth consignment for the Continent hijacked at gunpoint by a gang at Mountnessing, Essex, last May. Detectives do not know, it is understood, the identity of the second man involved in the shootings.

The wanted men did not see the story.

Essex police sat on the names for a couple of days. While they were doing so there was an unexpected new development: Len White pulled his men out of the Barn, which had been the centre of their investigations for two weeks. He interrupted a Press conference that Patience was giving on Tuesday November 21. 'Gentlemen,' he began, 'there is a lot of stuff which Mr Patience is telling you which will seriously impede our inquiries. I can't stop him talking to you but I can only ask you to be discreet.'

Patience had been relating the story of how he was warned

of the possible attack on the Barn (at least six months before it had happened), but White's real objection was that Ince's name had leaked out to reporters. Patience had exasperated the police, not least because he had declared his intentions of selling his family's horror story to the *Sunday Mirror*. 'It all adds up to LSD,' he said later. The police persuaded him to drop the idea.

After the conference, White had a private talk with Patience; the result was that the police moved their headquarters from the Barn into the more cramped – and certainly less luxurious – surroundings of the local police station at Braintree. Patience had clearly had enough. 'I don't want anything more to do with the police – and I don't want you round me any more either,' he snapped at one of the reporters. The Essex murder squad were shortly to receive a bill from the Barn for 1680 cups of coffee, 200 pints of milk, 374 lunches and 130 sandwiches. Lunch cost, at that time, 60p and coffee 8p a cup.

But the rift between Patience and the police was more than just a barney over coffee and sandwiches. The police had at one time worked on the theory that Ince's friends Matthews, Sims and Molloy had stolen the bullion and hidden it in the disused swimming pool near the Barn. This theory was later discounted and has since been treated as a huge joke by Patience. Less than eighteen months later he was running tombolas at the Barn with mock-up horse race cards. The 10.15 on the night of April 1, 1974, was entitled 'The Silver Bullion Hunt, sponsored by Bob Patience. Distance: three times round the perimeter of the swimming pool.' Patience thought that was hilarious, and proudly shows visitors the race card.

Ince heard that he was wanted for the murder by chance. On Wednesday November 22 he phoned his mother from Kent. His sister Phyllis answered the phone. She was tense and emotional. She said he was wanted for the Barn murder. The police had been round and, she told him, they had guns. What was he going to do? Ince was calm on the phone. He told Phyllis not to worry, to leave everything to him, and he replaced the receiver.

Ince knew he was in very serious trouble. If the police were hunting for him they would find him eventually. It was not as though they were looking for a man to give evidence in an important trial, or hunting a bullion robber. In the search for a suspected murderer they would mobilize all their resources. And Ince knew that a suspected murderer who was successful for weeks in avoiding the police could easily confirm his guilt in the eyes of the public. But he was not guilty, and he knew that his best hope of convincing the police of that fact was to avoid going to ground or going on the run.

Ince decided almost immediately to come into the open. He tried to telephone his solicitor, George Stanley, but he was out, so he decided to leave everything for twenty-four hours and think about his situation. He reckoned he knew what he had been doing on the night of the murder. If it had been a Saturday it was likely that he had been with Dolly, but he wasn't sure. He telephoned her the next morning. She remembered at once, because it had been Guy Fawkes weekend: she knew that George had been with her throughout that Saturday night.

At that stage Ince anticipated no trouble in convincing the police of his innocence. Just by giving himself up he was showing he had nothing to fear. But his was not a spotless record; he could not be sure what attitude the police would adopt. A thief does not give himself up – especially if he knows he is wanted for a robbery. Yet murder is the ultimate crime. Violence may often be the order of the day for a robbery and men may become heroes through a bravely or cunningly executed theft, but the murderer is never a hero – especially the one who kills in the calculating way of the killer of Muriel Patience. Ince knew, as Len White knew, that it was this type of murder that can turn the most solid friends into police informers. Ince was not prepared to risk that. He would give himself up and quickly establish his innocence.

Ince asked Mrs Grey if she would go to see his solicitor and make a statement providing his alibi for the night of the murder. He was reluctant to involve her, but she was the only person who could provide the alibi, and anyway Ince was sure it would be a matter only between Mrs Grey, the police and his solicitor. He could not, at that stage, envisage the case going any further, certainly not to trial. Before he gave himself up, Ince also considered making a statement of his innocence to a Sunday newspaper, and an approach was made to the *Sunday Times* without his identity being revealed. The paper showed interest, but in the end Ince decided against it. He had been told that armed policemen were hunting for him, and he was scared. He was advised to disappear for the weekend. Mrs Grey made her statement to Stanley, and Ince arranged to meet him the following Monday morning, November 27.

Over that weekend, Essex police continued to confirm the identification of Ince with Beverley. From a search of Ince's flat they had found a coloured snapshot of him standing on a rocky cliff somewhere near the sea. On Saturday November 24 – three weeks after the shootings – they showed Beverley a black-and-white enlargement of this colour snap. She looked at it through a magnifying glass, and again identified Ince as the gunman – the fourth time she had made positive identification. Her father, on the other hand, had consistently failed to associate pictures of Ince with his recollections of the murderer, a trend that was to continue. On the same day Detective Constable Griffiths took the album of photographs marked 'A' to show Bunny Layzell. He picked out No. 3 – Ince.

Ince stayed the night of November 26 with a friend in London. Next morning he caught a Central Line underground train to Theydon Bois, entering Essex police territory. Outside the tube station he met Stanley, who was sitting in his car. Ince got into the front passenger seat beside his solicitor.

Together they prepared a statement in which Ince denied having anything to do with the murder and said he could provide independent evidence to confirm that he was elsewhere at the time. They drove to Epping and parked the car outside the police station. The few steps Ince took from Stanley's car into Epping police station were his last as a free man for a very long time. Within twelve hours he was to be charged with murder.

5 · The case against George Ince

While Ince and Stanley were sitting outside Theydon Bois underground station preparing the statement, a colleague of Stanley's telephoned Braintree police station. Detective Inspector Toller took the call. He talked for a few minutes then turned to the other officers in the room. Ince was giving himself up, he told them excitedly.

The caller had told Toller that Ince would be arriving at Epping police station. The Braintree station contacted Epping to warn them to expect an important visitor. When Ince and Stanley walked in ten minutes later, just after noon, Chief Inspector Wilfred Newnham was expecting them. 'I am arresting you in connection with the murder inquiry at Braintree,' he said immediately to Ince. 'I understand,' Ince replied.

Stanley then produced Ince's unsigned statement and an accompanying letter. He wanted his client to sign the statement in front of Newnham. Newnham read it, and gave it back to Stanley. He said it was not something for him to handle, and he would prefer it if the matter was left until the detectives arrived from Braintree. He phoned Braintree to tell them their wanted man was in custody. Ince was put in a cell and Stanley sat in the waiting room.

Detective Chief Superintendent Len White sent his number two, Detective Superintendent George Harris, and two other detectives to Epping to collect Ince. Their car arrived at Epping at about 12.30 pm. Harris saw Ince and checked that he had already been cautioned. He saw Stanley, who gave him the statement. Harris read it, seemingly unimpressed. Ince told Harris that he had given himself up because he had heard from his sister that he was wanted for the Barn murder. He was absolutely innocent and he could prove he was elsewhere at the time. Harris replied that Ince would be taken to Braintree and interviewed there, and later that day he would take part in an identification parade. Ince just answered: 'Yes.' Little was said at that stage. At 1.55 the police car driven by Detective Inspector Wyatt left Epping for Braintree. Harris sat in the front, with Ince in the back next to Detective Constable Micky Lewis. Stanley went in his own car.

At first there was complete silence, but then some rather strained conversation began. Ince remembers that during the thirty-mile drive Wyatt told him he would be charged with the murder. He also says Lewis was armed (which is not surprising, since the police believed they were dealing with a dangerous gunman).

Harris made a note of his recollection of the conversation during the drive. He recalls that Wyatt said to Ince: 'You do know where you're going, don't you?' Ince asked him where, and when told he was going to Braintree said he had never been there.

'What made you suddenly start looking for me for this job?' Ince asked.

'You'll hear all about it when you get to Braintree,' said Harris.

'This shooting happened on my manor,' interjected Wyatt with some pride.

There was a long pause and then Wyatt asked: 'Whatever made you give yourself up, and why at Epping?'

'Because I never did it.'

'Why at Epping?' repeated Wyatt.

'It's the nearest nick in Essex.'

'I think it's because you heard we were armed and you didn't want to take the chance of being shot.'

'There's your answer. You've said it for me.'

Harris joined in. 'I think you're a bit of a gambler, aren't you?' he said to Ince.

'I bet quite a bit. Why?'

'I reckon this is a bit of a gamble, that's why.'

'What do you mean?'

'We have been looking for you. As soon as you hear we want you for the shooting, then suddenly you give yourself up. That's the gamble, on not being identified, and then you avoid the danger of any evidence being found when you are picked up unexpectedly.'

'Rubbish. I just didn't want to get done for killing anyone.'

But Harris seriously reckoned that Ince *was* taking a gamble on not being picked out on the identity parade. He then turned the conversation to the Mountnessing bullion robbery by remarking on Ince's tan and asking him if he had been with his mates Sims and Molloy: 'We have been trying to trace all of you since May.' Ince refused to be drawn. 'You know I'm not going to tell you anything,' he said. Harris tried to loosen him up and started talking about cars, mentioning that Ince used to have a Volkswagen. Wyatt interjected: 'The car the gunmen used was a Volkswagen. It belonged to David Patience.'

'I don't know what you're talking about,' Ince replied.

As the police car drove past Great Leighs, just a few miles short of Braintree, Wyatt remarked that the fishing was good round there. He asked Ince if he had ever fished in the area. Ince said he had never been there before. He would not bite. He knew what the police wanted, and he was determinedly unhelpful, moody and reticent. He didn't want to talk at all. He was thinking about what awaited him in Braintree, the interviews and the identification parades which were to follow.

The car drew up at Braintree police station at about 3 pm. At 4.20 Ince met Len White for the first time. That first encounter was brief: the main, long questioning took place an hour and a half later.

At 5.55 that afternoon, in an upstairs room at Braintree police station, Ince was formally interviewed by White. The two men sat on either side of a table. Beside White sat Harris, who was taking down the interview, and Wyatt. Stanley sat next to Ince, and just behind Ince was Lewis. The interview lasted for an hour and twenty minutes. White cautioned Ince, told him he was being interviewed because he was suspected of being one of two men responsible for the Barn shootings, and reminded him he was not obliged to say anything.

Ince said that he had been at the Whitstable caravan site for the last few months and that he had seen Sims, Molloy and Matthews while he had been there. He had never been to the

Barn and had never met Robert, Muriel, David or Beverley Patience. 'Therefore,' said White, 'what is your reply regarding the crimes I have mentioned above?'

Ince replied: 'I am absolutely innocent and that is what I have come to see you about.'

He admitted that he had once possessed a pistol, but he had never fired it. He had it, he said, for his own protection because he had been shot twice. He had thrown it into the River Lea in Hackney some fifteen months previously.

White asked where he had been on November 4, and Stanley then passed to White an envelope containing the statements from Ince and Mrs Doris Grey.

White read Ince's statement:

> On Wednesday the 22nd November I telephoned my mother and my sister, who lives with my mother at her address, told me that police officers had called inquiring for me and saying they wanted to interview me with regard to the Braintree murder, which I took to mean the incidents relating to a Mr and Mrs Bob Patience.
>
> I have never to my knowledge met either Mr Bob Patience or his wife or his daughter and am therefore not acquainted with any of them, and neither have I previously heard of them. I know nothing whatsoever of the events relating to Mr Patience and his family and am perfectly willing to assist police in their inquiries into this matter, and I do not know why they have called at my mother's address asking to interview me in regard to this matter.
>
> When I heard of this incident I endeavoured to contact my solicitors and was able to do so on Thursday the 23rd November and have thereafter acted upon their advice, and in pursuance of that advice is it my intention to make myself available to police for the purpose of answering any questions which I may be able to answer in regard to this matter and to give every assistance which they think I may be able to afford them, and if required to attend any identification proceedings, although I repeat that I know nothing whatever of the incident or of the persons concerned in it.
>
> On the night of Saturday the 4th November I was in London

and have independent evidence to support this fact, and can recall the date because it was fireworks night and also because I heard of the Braintree murder during the Sunday following the Saturday 4th November.

This is all I am able to say regarding this matter except that I have also been advised by my legal advisers that I am not to discuss any matters or answer any questions of whatsoever nature unless and until they are afforded an opportunity of being present during any such proposed interrogation for the purpose of avoiding any future dispute or misunderstanding which might arise during that interrogation, and I intend adopting that advice and not answering any questions unless and until a representative from my legal advisers is present.

On the night of Saturday 4th/Sunday 5th November, to the best of my recollection, I was wearing a two-piece blue/grey single-breasted suit with a faint red stripe in it, together with a mauve-coloured shirt and blue tie with mauve diagonal pattern, together with black shoes, but I am unable to specify which particular pair.

White then read the alibi, the statement of Mrs Doris Grey:

I have known a man named George Ince for some considerable years past and we formed an intimate association. I have been in the habit of seeing him from time to time and the last occasion on which I saw him was on the night of Saturday 4th and Sunday 5th November last, this being Guy Fawkes night.

I had been to my mother's flat which is nearby and had a meal with her and left around 8 pm together with my daughter aged seven, and we arrived home soon after 8 pm. I also have a son aged twenty-one who was just going out for the evening. I collected some fireworks and went downstairs and used these up for the benefit of my baby daughter and round about 8.30 pm went upstairs to the flat and I can well recall this incident.

Soon after this George Ince called, and I would say it was somewhere after 8.30 but before 9 pm, and he came into the flat and I made a cup of tea and we sat talking together, and also looked at television for the rest of the evening. George Ince stayed the night and we slept together, and he had a cup of tea in the morning and left somewhere between 9 am and 10 am as nearly as I can fix it. I am certain that he spent the hours of 9 pm on Saturday 4th November until 9 am on Sunday 5th November with me in my flat, and of this I have no doubt and am able to fix the dates because of that particular weekend and the fireworks I let off for my little daughter. I have not seen George Ince since that time.

My son telephoned that evening to say that he was going to his grandmother's in the City as he was in that direction and intended staying the night with her as it was a bit late for him to try to get home, and it was in fact late when he telephoned. I was not surprised at this because occasionally he does stay with his grandmother at weekends, in which event he telephones and lets me know, as he did on this occasion.

I am a married woman and I appreciate the difficulty of my position but I have been asked whether or not I could confirm that George Ince did stay with me on this night, and as in fact he did I have decided to tell the truth, and what I have said is the absolute truth and this statement has been made by me quite voluntarily.

Doris Grey had added a supplementary statement:

I wish to say further that I have made this and my previous statement because George Ince telephoned me and told me that he intended voluntarily surrendering himself for police questioning because he had heard that they wanted to see him, and asked me if I recalled the evening of Saturday 4th/Sunday 5th November, and if I did whether I would go to his solicitors and make a statement to that effect, which I have done.

George Ince has stayed at my flat on previous occasions but the 4th/5th November was the last occasion and I have not seen him since, and I have particular reason for remembering that weekend.

There had been silence while White was reading through the statements. He finished and looked up. He suggested that even if the statements were true it was possible that Ince might have slipped away while Mrs Grey was asleep and still been able to go to the Barn. Stanley prevented Ince from answering those sort of questions; he called them conjecture. White asked where Mrs Grey's husband was that night. It was of course a crucial question. After insisting that this information would not be included in the report of the interview, and being assured by White that it would not be, Stanley told White that Mrs Grey's husband was Charles Kray and that he was in Maidstone prison.

White put the statements down. 'This will make a lovely story in the papers,' he said, according to Ince. White looked at him and smiled. Ince knew what he meant: producing Charlie Kray's wife as an alibi was hardly the most powerful argument in the world for persuading the police that he was elsewhere.

White questioned Ince in detail about the night he spent with Dolly, and about what he did that Saturday before he went round to Dolly's. That stage of the interview finished at 7.15 pm with White saying: 'Do you appreciate that although you have said who you were with that night and that you can even describe happenings at her home, the police recognize it still could have been possible for you then to drive to Braintree arriving just before 2 am and commit these crimes?'

Stanley answered for Ince: 'I appreciate the reasoning but I do not accept it.'

Ince was then put into a police car and driven to Colchester police station, fifteen miles away. He had said in the original statement he had prepared with Stanley that he was quite ready to take part in identity parades; it was for that reason he was taken to Colchester.

Ince was about to have his first confrontation with the Patience family. He was hoping that within an hour or so, after everybody had failed to identify him, the police would realize that he had nothing to do with the murder and he would be released. But he was not altogether confident that that would in fact be the outcome. He had heard Harris talking about the bullion robbery, and he knew there would be more questions to be answered on that matter. But if he could get the murder off his mind then at least he would sleep reasonably that night. The next couple of hours sealed his fate and induced in him a feeling of inner panic: a fear that he would never be able to convince the police of his innocence.

The events of that Monday evening, and the fact that it was subsequently established that Ince was not the murderer, call seriously into question the validity of the identification parade as a means of determining whether or not a man has taken part in a crime. But the ID parade is an everyday tool of the detective's trade, and there is a strict procedure laid down in a Home Office circular to the police. (This circular is reproduced in full in the Appendix.) In short, parades are expected to be carried out in accordance with the following rules:

> That the police officer in charge of the parade is of a rank not lower than inspector.
>
> That, once the parade has been formed, all matters such as instructions to the witnesses should be carried out in front of the suspect.
>
> That the witnesses should not see the suspect before the parade, and that those who have seen photographs of the suspect before the parade should not be led into identifying the suspect because they remember the photograph.
>
> That the other people making up the parade with the suspect should be of the same age, height, general appearance, standard of dress and position in life as the suspect.
>
> That the suspect is allowed to choose where he stands in the line, is allowed to object to anybody else standing in the line with him, and is allowed to have a solicitor or friend in the room when the parade is being conducted.
>
> That the witnesses come in one at a time, and that the suspect is told that he can change his position in the line after each witness has left, if he wants to.
>
> That the witness should be told that if he cannot make a positive identification he should say so, but that if he can he should touch the person he believes he can identify.
>
> That if he thinks he can identify somebody, but is not sure, he should tell the police officer in charge of the parade, who should note this carefully.

That if the witness wants the members of the parade to walk or speak or carry out some other action to help in the identification there should be no objection to this, but it should be recorded by the officer in charge.

The five key eye-witnesses called by the police to Colchester police station that Monday evening were all supposed to have seen the man who shot Muriel Patience twenty-two days before. Four of them waited together in the Detective Chief Inspector's office on the top floor of the police station before the parade. When Ince arrived with White and Stanley he was kept apart on the ground floor.

In charge of the identification parade was Chief Inspector James Gorham, from Braintree. He assembled the members of the parade in a hall in the station. At 8.30 Ince was brought into the hall. Stanley was present throughout. Ince looked at the other eight men who were to stand in the line with him, and he asked them all to take off their jackets. He noticed that he was the only one of the nine who was wearing a white shirt and knew that would make him stand out, so he changed shirts with his solicitor, Stanley, putting on his pale biscuit-coloured one. He joined the line third from the left. Stanley noticed that Ince had a small scar on his right cheek, and thought that this might make him stand out on the parade, so he asked Gorham whether a piece of sticking plaster could be used to cover it. This was supplied, and every other man on the parade also had a small piece of plaster stuck to his right cheek.

The witnesses were briefed by Gorham. He told them to say if they were not one hundred per cent certain when making an identification, to take as long as they liked, and to study each man very carefully. The first witness at 8.40 was the most important one: Beverley Patience. She had spent longest with the gunman; she had been close to him in a brightly-lit room for half an hour or so. It must be stressed also that she had seen several photographs of Ince before she went on the parade and had positively identified him as the murderer. She entered the room from the left-hand side, nearest to number one in the line, and walked along, looking intently at the face of each man standing there staring straight ahead. She had walked only as far as the fifth man in the line when she stopped, turned back, and touched the third man, Ince, on the shoulder. Then she left the room.

Ince felt totally numbed. Gorham asked him, as he did after each witness had left the room, whether he wanted to change position in the line, but he said he would stay where he was.

Bob Patience, the next witness, came into the room at 8.45. He too had been in the room with the gunman for around twenty minutes on the night of the shootings. He too had seen pictures of Ince before but had not positively identified him. He was, in theory, the police's second most important witness, and he spent much longer examining the men on the identification parade than had his daughter. He walked along the front of the line of men, stopping in front of each one and staring at him. Then he went behind the line and walked along, again stopping behind each man. He came back to the front and asked Gorham if the men on the parade could point their right hands as though they were holding guns, and if they could then say 'I want the key to the safe,' just as the gunman had in the Sun Lido House. One at a time, the nine men did as Patience had asked. Patience walked along the front of the line again. He stopped in front of Ince, stared at him again, and then walked on down the line and stopped in front of the last man. He said: 'I think it is this man.' Patience left the room at 8.50 pm. The man he had picked out was a bigger man than Ince, and had a more sallow face, darker hair, and heavy eyebrows.

The next witness, at 8.52 pm, was David Patience, who had caught a fleeting glimpse of the gunman and his accomplice as they drove out of the Barn car park in his car. David had seen a lot of photographs between the murder and the identification parade. In particular, he remembered seeing some photographs in White's office about eight or nine days before the identification parade; they were of the man called Derek Davies, who had phoned him and claimed that he knew who had committed the murder. David had not been shown pictures of Ince before the parade, although he might have seen them lying around the incidents room at the Barn restaurant. He walked along the line of nine men and then asked Gorham if he could see the men seated as though in a car. Chairs were brought up and the men sat down. David walked back down the line and went up to Ince, still third in the line. He touched him on the shoulder saying: 'I am not one hundred per cent certain but I think it could be this man.'

After he had left the parade David went to another room in the police station where he chatted with his father and sister. He later told the magistrates court that when he picked out Ince and told Gorham he was not one hundred per cent certain it was because he had been told to say if he was not absolutely sure. But he also told the magistrates court:

'Before I left Colchester police station that night I made a further statement. We had to make a statement after attending the identification parade. At the time I left the identification parade at Colchester police station I was in a much happier mood, because the investigation was moving forward and I had identified somebody. I had by that time further thoughts about my identification on the parade and by the time I made my statement I had come to the conclusion that I was one hundred per cent certain that the man I had identified was the man that I had seen in the passenger seat of my car.'

David Patience's statement at Colchester police station was timed at 10.20 pm, an hour and a half after he had picked Ince out on the parade, a few minutes after the parade had finally ended. David said in this statement:

'Although after identifying him I said "I am not one hundred per cent certain but I think this is the man", I am now completely positive. Particularly as I also recognize him now as the man I know as George Ince and who I met casually in Jersey about five years ago at my father's birthday party. It was not until I saw him in the parade at Colchester police station that I realized that George Ince and the man in the passenger seat of the Volkswagen were identical. I have now no doubt whatsoever that George Ince was the man in the passenger seat of the Volkswagen.'

Later David retracted the claim that he had met Ince before in Jersey. It had been a mistake. He had never met Ince before.

Ince changed position in the parade for the first time, to fifth in the line, when Jonathan Ridley, the retired serviceman who had been asked the way in Braintree by two men, came into the parade at 9.04 pm. He was in the room only a few moments. He walked along the front of the line, looking at the nine men, and then walked back down the front of the line and out of the room. He said nothing and identified no one.

The last witness was to be Bunny Layzell, the lorry-driver who had been in the Chequers Hotel in Felsted and had seen two 'nasty types' in the bar on November 2. Layzell was late, and Gorham announced a break for refreshment. It was 9.15. The parade was re-formed at 10.10. Ince had decided to change shirts again. He took off Stanley's biscuit-coloured one and borrowed a green shirt from another of the men on the parade. This man put on Stanley's shirt. Ince joined the line at number five and at 10.15 Layzell came into the room. He walked up the line and back down again, went straight up to Ince and touched him on the shoulder.

The parade was over. Gorham asked Stanley and Ince if they had any objections to the conduct of the parade and both replied that they had not. White, who had been watching throughout the parade, said to Ince: 'You will be detained and subsequently formally charged with the murder of Mrs Muriel Patience. You are not obliged to say anything unless you wish to do so but what you say may be taken down and given in evidence.'

'The girl and the others have made a mistake,' was all Ince said.

The matter of the colour of Ince's shirt was to become a central issue when the case came to trial. At the start of the parade Ince was wearing his solicitor's shirt – a biscuit-coloured one – and he continued wearing this for the first four witnesses. He only changed into a green shirt, belonging to another man on the parade, for the last witness. This sequence is corroborated by Gorham's detailed account of the parade, as well as by Ince and Stanley. As we have seen Bob Patience did not pick out Ince. He thought the gunman looked like the man who was standing at No. 9. But outside the parade room he told a policeman that he had picked out the wrong man. He made a statement saying that he had studied, for some considerable time, the man standing third from the left, wearing a 'greenish shirt'. 'On leaving the parade,' he said in the statement, 'I realized that I had made a mistake and that it was the man I had hesitated over, the man standing in the line third from the left.' Ince was indeed standing third in line but he did not put on the green shirt until 10.10. Bob Patience had seen the parade at 8.45. His statement was timed at 10.30.

It was not until Ince's second murder trial that Gorham told the court that in his original report on the identification parade he had forgotten to mention that Ince changed his shirt on yet another occasion, with the first man in the line, who was also wearing a green shirt. It was a lapse of memory on Inspector Gorham's part which was exploited by the defence.

Ince was driven back to Braintree and at 11.40 he was again in the interview room with White and Harris. His answers to the questions earlier that evening were read over to him and he was also interrogated about the caravan site at Whitstable and what he had been doing on the Sunday of the murder. He told White that he had last seen Mrs Grey on that Sunday morning. The interview finished and Ince then signed each page of the record of his answers. He had been in custody for just over twelve hours when at 12.35 he was taken downstairs to the charge room. White read out Bob Patience's 'second-thoughts' statement and David Patience's 'now-I'm-sure' statement. Neither Ince nor Stanley said anything. Wyatt formally charged Ince with the murder of Muriel Patience. 'I don't wish to say anything,' said Ince. He was taken to a cell at Braintree station.

Later that Tuesday morning he appeared at Braintree magistrates court, but not until a few minutes before the hearing did the police release his name. His head was covered with a blanket as he was led into the court building, handcuffed and surrounded by policemen. Inside the court the security was equally strong. The dock was ringed with uniformed and plain-clothes policemen. There was even a detective among the members of the public in the gallery. Ince was dressed smartly in a grey suit, white shirt, and a dark-blue tie with a white embroidered motif. He stood in front of the three magistrates on the bench, staring straight ahead, and told the chairman of the magistrates that he was not guilty. Detective Chief Superintendent White's application for a three-day remand was granted, and Ince was taken away to the cells at Colchester police station. The hearing only lasted a few minutes.

Next day, Wednesday November 29, there was another identification parade at Colchester; again Gorham was in charge. It was held in the afternoon and three more witnesses were to see if they could pick out Ince from a total of nine men. Ince's solicitor was there. The first witness was Harry Leverett, who, along with Bunny Layzell, had seen the two strangers in the Chequers pub. He walked along the front of the line and quickly went up to Ince and touched him. 'I think this is the man,' he said.

The next witness was Arthur Lewis, landlord of the Cherry Tree pub in Rayne Road. He had served a pint of beer to a stranger, who appeared to be on his own, at about 9 o'clock on the night of the murder. He had been shown a number of photographs of suspects, and had said that the photograph of Ince looked very similar to the man in his pub that night, Lewis walked into the room where the parade was being held. walked along the line and back, and left the room without saying anything. He then made a statement saying that the man he had seen in his pub was definitely not on the parade.

The last witness was Renée Jarvis, Lewis's sister-in-law. She too had been in the Cherry Tree the night of the murder and had seen the stranger. She, too, had been shown photographs and had picked out one of Ince as bearing a close resemblance to the man she had seen. She walked along the identification parade and left the room shaking her head.

Those two parades, one on the 27th, the other on the 29th, were the only ones Ince attended in connection with the Barn murder. He had been seen by eight witnesses. Three of them, Beverley Patience, Bunny Layzell and Harry Leverett, had picked him out immediately. David Patience had picked him out but had not, at first, been totally sure. Bob Patience had picked out another man, but had later changed his mind and said he should have picked Ince. Jonathan Ridley, Arthur Lewis and Renée Jarvis had not picked out anyone.

On the Thursday of that week, the 30th, the police took a statement from a fifteen-year-old schoolboy called James Falkener, who claimed to have seen Ince in the Felsted area around the time of the murder. Falkener was a pupil at Felsted, a well-known public school, and he was in Felsted village on the Thursday before the murder, the 2nd, the same day the two strangers entered the Chequers pub.

At about four in the afternoon on that Thursday Falkener went into a newsagents' in the main street of Felsted. At the counter buying some cigarettes, was a man wearing a three-quarter length coat who, said Falkener, was behaving very furtively. He kept looking down, and when he left the shop he hurried out, brushing past Falkener as he went.

Nearly three weeks later, on Tuesday November 28, the Felsted schoolboys were asked to look at two photographs to help the police investigating the Barn murder. Had they seen the men in the photographs, they were asked. One of the pictures was of Ince, and Falkener said he was sure it was the same man he had seen in the newsagents' that Thursday afternoon. Two days later he made a statement saying he was certain it was the same man and that he would recognize him if he saw him again.

The police were still looking for the second man who went to the Barn on November 5, the one they thought of as the passive one, who had remained silent while the gunman shot Mrs Patience. Because they were convinced Ince was the gunman, they traced friends and acquaintances of his, looking for somebody who matched Beverley's rather vague description of the second man. They picked on two suspects. One was a London docker, John Brett, who was later, like Ince, sentenced to fifteen years imprisonment for the Mountnessing bullion robbery. The police announced that they wanted to see these two men.

They had a seven-year-old photograph of Brett which they thought matched Beverley's description of the second man, but Brett had changed enormously in that time. His hair was much longer and he had a moustache and a beard.

Brett heard that he was wanted in connection with the Barn murder and like Ince, knowing he had no part in the murder and anxious to clear himself, decided to give himself up. He telephoned his solicitor, Ralph Haeems, on Monday December 4, and asked for a meeting, but Haeems told him to come into his office the following morning. He did not want to take the risk of being seen with a wanted man, or of being thought to be harbouring. Brett walked into Haeems' office, made a statement, and said he wanted to give himself up.

Haeems knew that Detective Chief Superintendent Albert Wickstead (the man in charge of Scotland Yard's Serious Crimes Squad) was involved in the Tibbs trial at the Old Bailey that morning. He decided to surrender his client to him. Wickstead arranged for another policeman to take Brett to Braintree and hand him over to the Essex police. Haeems went with him.

Later that Tuesday the identification parade for the second Barn raider was held at Colchester police station. Gorham was again in charge, and Brett was one of eleven men standing in the line. He chose to stand second from the left. The police asked him if he would be prepared to shave off his beard. Brett refused. He had had his beard for several weeks; he had certainly had it two weeks previously when the Barn shootings happened; he did not intend to change his appearance to help the police by making himself more like the description of the gunman's accomplice. Other men with beards had to be found for the parade.

None of the descriptions of the second man included any mention of a beard; it is thus surprising to say the least that the police saw fit to put Brett on an identification parade, and even more surprising that he was picked out. Clearly the police believed that his beard was not as old as he claimed, and hoped that other facial features would stand out through it.

Beverley Patience was the first witness. She walked right along the line and back again, staring hard at each man. She walked along again and stopped at the man in the tenth position.

George Ince

The Patience family – David, Muriel, Bob and Beverley – at the Cavalier Bar in the Barn restaurant

Sun Lido House, the Patience family home near the Barn where the shootings took place

The Barn restaurant

Bob Patience's visiting card: colour photograph of him holding a list of the ures of Abraham Lincoln

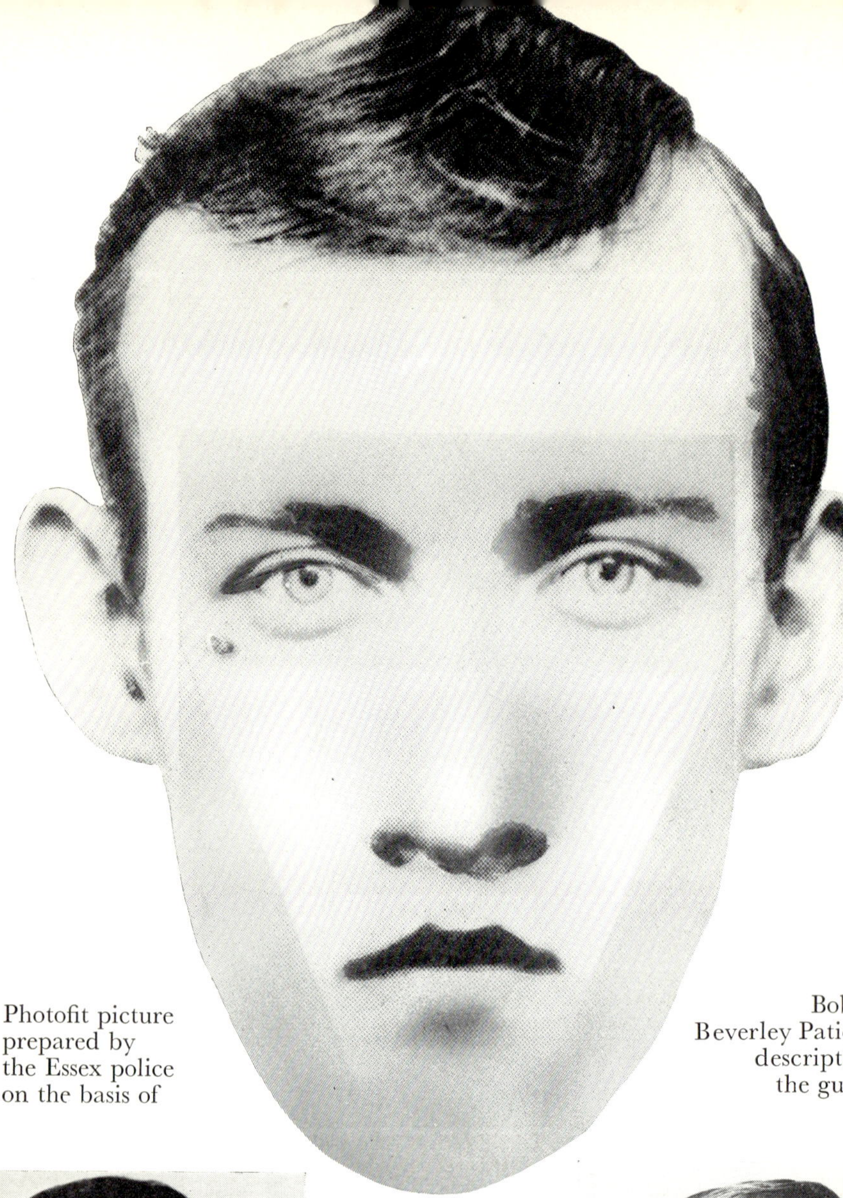

Photofit picture prepared by the Essex police on the basis of

Bob Beverley Patien descriptio the gun

Two pictures of George Ince: (left) passport photograph taken in 1971 and included on the card of twelve shown to Beverley in hospital; and a photograph taken in November 1972 after he had given himself up

John Brook, convicted in January 1974 of the murder of Muriel Patience, and now serving a life-sentence

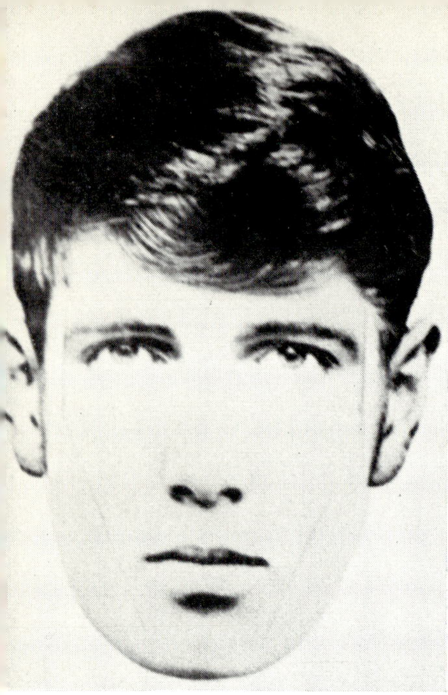

Photofit picture of
the gunman's accomplice
prepared by the Essex police
on the basis of descriptions
provided by Bob and Beverley
Patience, and
Nicholas de Clare Johnson,
who admitted to his presence
at the Barn,
was convicted of manslaughter
and is now serving ten years

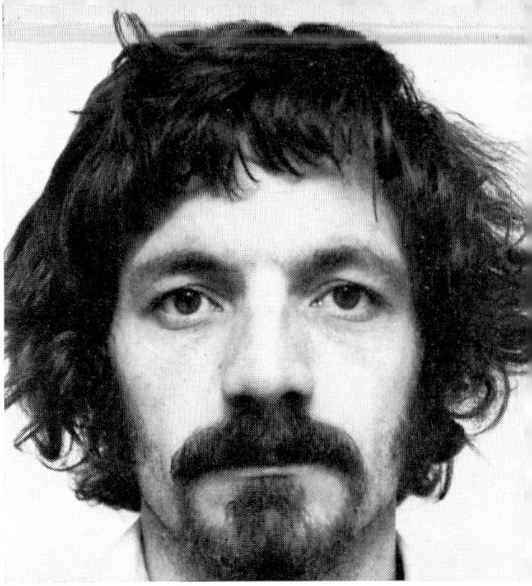

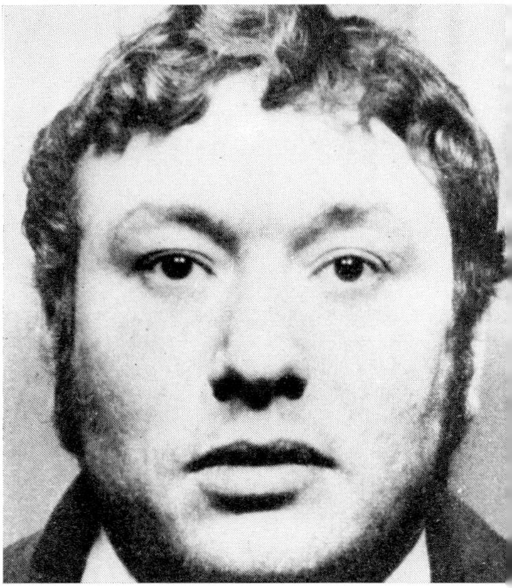

Ronald Molloy, John Brett, and Francis Sims – the three men convicted with Ince in November 1973 of the Mountnessing silver bullion robbery. All are serving fifteen-year sentences.

Below, Charles Matthews, who was acquitted

George Ince's mother Minnie with her daughters (left to right) Phyllis, Pauline, Margaret, Betty and Rose

She touched him and left the room. This man was an innocent volunteer.

Brett remained at number two and Bob Patience came in. As usual he took longer examining the men on the parade than anyone else. He stopped in front of each man, stared hard, and then moved on to the next. He walked along the back of the line doing the same. Twice more he walked along the front of the line, and finally he stopped in front of Brett and touched him.

David Patience came in next. As he had done with Ince, he asked the members of the parade to sit down as though they were in a car. As his sister had done, David Patience picked out the tenth man.

Bunny Layzell asked everybody on the parade to hold both hands out, palms down, and examined their hands very carefully. Finally he touched the first man in the line, another innocent member of the public. Harry Leverett came in next and identified the same man.

John Pickering, who was supposed to have seen two men in Felsted on the Thursday before the murder, took quite some time. He walked along the line three times and then stood in the middle staring at each man in turn. Finally he touched the tenth man. Mrs Lund, who also saw two men in Felsted, was much quicker; she went straight up to the tenth man and touched him. The parade was over. Brett had been identified by only one person, Bob Patience. Two men chosen at random to make up the parade had been identified, one four times and the other twice, as the murderer's accomplice at the Barn on November 5. The parade was meaningless. Brett was not charged.

Shortly afterwards, the police put up their second suspect for the gunman's accomplice, whom we shall call Mr X. His friendship with Ince seems the only possible reason to have involved him. Mr X had in fact been in India at the time of the murder, but the police had only accepted that after he had been on an identification parade. On December 14 he took part in an identification parade at Colchester police station. There were four witnesses, the three members of the Patience family and Harry Leverett. Bob and Beverley Patience both picked out the man who was standing second in the line. He was an innocent member of the public. David Patience and Leverett picked no one. Mr X was eliminated.

The final parade for the second man was held in Colchester on January 24, 1973: the suspect was another friend of Ince's, Mr Y. The three Patiences, Layzell, Leverett and Joseph Ripton, the landlord of the Chequers, were the witnesses. Beverley and her father both picked out one volunteer; David picked out another; Layzell a third and Ripton a fourth. Only Leverett picked out Mr Y. All the witnesses had picked someone out of the nine men taking part in the parade; but the suspect had been picked out only once. Mr Y was also eliminated.

While the parades were being held an extraordinary thing happened to Bob Patience. On January 4 he went to Braintree court to make a routine application for a licence for his restaurant, and by a remarkable coincidence found himself sitting in court with Ince once again in the dock. The police were seeking a further remand. Patience sat down in the back of the court to wait for his own matter to be dealt with, and during that time, he said afterwards, he gazed at the back of the head of the man in the dock. He only saw Ince's face when he left the court.

Patience was now convinced that Ince was the man who shot his wife. He later told the magistrates court: 'I was convinced one hundred per cent that the colour of the hair, the hairstyle, the shape of the head, was identical to the man who leant over my wife on that night and said, "She will be all right." On the occasion of the first identification parade that I had attended I thought that the hairstyle was different. On the 4th January, in this court room, everything was identical.' The police now believed that they had a strong case against Ince. The two survivors who had spent a considerable time with the gunman in the room where Mrs Patience was shot were both saying that they were sure he was the man.

An analysis of the Patiences' performances in a series of identification parades appears in Chapter 10. That their powers of recall were unreliable, since they had picked out a number of people from identification parades who could not possibly have had any connection with the murder, must have suggested itself to the police. Nevertheless, details of the case were sent to the Director of Public Prosecutions, who agreed that Ince had a case to answer. He appeared before the Braintree magistrates for the last time on March 9 and was committed for trial at Chelmsford Crown Court the following May. He spent the intervening time in Brixton prison.

6 - To catch a thief . . .

RONALD MOLLOY, Frankie Sims and Chic Matthews dealt in scrap metal. At the beginning of November 1972 they won a demolition contract to remove disused railway lines from a siding at Angerstine Wharf in Greenwich. But they had only been working there for a month when they had to call the operation off. It was December 4. Sims and Matthews had been loading the lines on to a truck; it had been raining and by midday they were wet through. They decided to stop work. They got into a white Austin 1100 and drove to R & N Motors, a car dealers in Blackwell Lane, just round the corner from the wharf. As they approached the garage they noticed groups of men standing in the showroom. There were several cars parked outside and although they were unmarked both Sims and Matthews 'smelt' the police. Sims knew that he and Molloy had been named by Golly Sillett as two of the men who had taken part in the bullion robbery: it seemed as though the police were closing in.

The two men stopped their car opposite the garage for a few seconds just to get a better look and, now certain that the men were police, drove away quickly, dumping their car a little later on the forecourt of a pub. They then phoned Molloy, who had not in fact turned up for work that morning because of the rain, to tell him what had happened. He agreed that they would have to 'disappear' again.

The three men had not been sleeping at their homes for the past seven months. After their holiday in the Margate hotel they had split up: Sims and Ince had gone to live in a caravan in Whitstable, where Matthews was also staying; Molloy had gone elsewhere. It was just a week after Ince had given himself up and had been charged with the Barn murder. The men knew that Ince had also been named by Sillett and they figured that the bullion inquiry was the likely reason for this renewed police activity. But, on the other hand, it could also be connected with the trial of the Tibbs family; the police might be looking for more witnesses. It had been the police search for men who were prepared to testify against the Tibbses that had kept Matthews out of London all summer.

Since the beginning of 1972 Scotland Yard's gangbusting squad, under the energetic leadership of Albert Wickstead, an East Ender by origin, had been rooting out reluctant witnesses against Jimmy Tibbs, the father, his three sons and some of their friends. They were wanted for crimes of violence. Matthews was an obvious choice for Wickstead. He had been a partner of Jimmy Tibbs in his scrap-metal business in Ordnance Road, Canning Town. Sims had been manager of a transport café which Tibbs and Matthews had opened next to the yard. Molloy had also worked with the Tibbs on scrap contracts over a number of years.

The day after they had seen the police at R & N Motors, Matthews and Sims established, through contacts in the Greenwich area, that on Tuesday December 5 the police had been waiting for them all day at the car sale-rooms. The police were unlucky there, but they had an unexpected breakthrough when the young docker, John Brett, gave himself up. Brett's surrender was described in the *Evening Standard* for December 6, but with an additional twist. The headline read: BARN KILLING: HUNT FOR 3 'VIOLENT' MEN. The story went on:

> South London and Kent police searched today for three men wanted for questioning in the Barn Restaurant killing of Mrs Muriel Patience. One of the three men police want to see is known to be driving a white Austin 1100. Aged 28, his home is in the Custom House area of East London. [That was Chic Matthews.] A second man, aged 47, comes from Rainham, Essex. When last seen he was at the wheel of a dark blue Ford Cortina. [Ronald Molloy.] The third man, aged 33, and born at Stratford comes from Forest Gate. [Frankie Sims.] Scotland Yard warned police in London today that all three men were extremely violent.

At 10.10 pm that day Brett was formally charged, not with the murder – or anything to do with it – but with the silver bullion robbery. 'I am completely innocent,' he told the Essex detectives, 'and I know nothing whatsoever of this matter.'

That evening Matthews telephoned Molloy again. He was so worried about the murder link in the report that he was going to phone a senior officer in the case, Detective Superintendent George Harris, at Brentwood. He did this at 7.30 pm from a callbox in Wanstead. When Harris answered, Matthews said that he was the man from Canning Town they were looking for: he was also speaking for the man from Stratford. Furthermore, he could find the man from Rainham, but he added: 'I want to be sure there is going to be no skulduggery, because if there is I'm not staying on the phone.' He was agitated: it had taken five minutes to get through to Harris and the police might be checking where the call was coming from. Although he intended to surrender himself to the police he was not prepared to do it without a solicitor, and would not tell Harris where he could be contacted.

Harris, to Matthews's amazement, said he was busy at that moment and could Matthews ring back in an hour. Matthews didn't know what to think. Perhaps the report in the *Evening Standard* had been incorrect. It seemed a funny way of dealing with an 'extremely violent man'. But he needed to cover himself. To avoid being picked up without a solicitor he drove out to Dagenham, in Essex, and waited until 9 o'clock before telephoning Harris again.

As Matthews picked up the receiver in the callbox and dialled Chelmsford 53131 he was sure that his conversation would either be taped or there would be someone listening in. He was very careful in choosing what he said to Harris and deliberately mentioned the reasons why he had been away from home – because he had been receiving threats; because Mr Wickstead's men had been looking for him. He was quite certain that he made particular reference to the Tibbses during the call. According to the police the call began at nine minutes past nine, at exactly the time that John Brett was being interrogated at Brentwood. What follows is the transcript which was presented as part of the prosecution case in the bullion trial.

Matthews: I was going to ask you, you can't believe everything you read in the papers, but what actually did you want me for Mr Harris?

Harris: Well, you know what we have been looking for you for for a long time. You have been in touch with your wife?

Matthews: Pardon?

Harris: You've been in touch with your wife?

Matthews: Yes, I did earlier.

Harris: So has Frankie. So has Ronnie with his family.

Matthews: Yeah.

Harris: You all know what you are wanted for.

Matthews: This is all water under the bridge, you know.

Harris: Obviously in time you will want to be seen.

Matthews: Yeah.

Harris: But there is a direct implication. You know who has been charged with the murder at Braintree don't you?

Matthews: Yes, I appreciate.

Harris: That is without me getting you to admit anything on the phone. You needn't answer this at all.

Matthews: No, I know.

Harris: But I know you are an associate of his.

Matthews: Yes.

Harris: Certain explanations have been made.

Matthews: Yeah.

Harris: Which necessitates you being seen.

Matthews: I appreciate that, yes.

Harris: Because he has been charged with an extremely violent murder.

Matthews: I appreciate that, yes.

Harris: And in this respect it may be that either one of you, or all three of you, are in a position to assist inquiries being conducted by Chief Superintendent White and myself from Braintree in respect of that murder.

Matthews: Yes.

Harris: There is another man who is wanted for that murder, as you will appreciate if you have read the newspapers.

Matthews: Yeah, well you can't believe everything that you read in the newspapers.

Harris: Well, this was committed by two men actually at the house.

Matthews: Yeah, I know that.

Harris: And possibly with another man.

Matthews: Yeah, that is what we are frightened of to be honest. I will be honest with you. You have been honest with me that there ain't no fit-up for this man outside or something.

Harris: There will not be a fit-up in quotes as you put it. I assure you of that. You will be dealt with according to the law. I have assured your families all along that there will be no fit-up. But if you have evidence against you in respect of the other offence [the murder] and explanations that you want to give, well that is a matter that you will have to deal with.

Matthews: Yeah. All I am worried about, I mean whoever did this is a crank, you appreciate this. You must know how it is rigged. We are not like other people you know.

Harris: Well, there are silly bits and pieces, Chic, which I won't go into, but I have no doubt . . .

Matthews: That ain't none of our game to be honest, you know that.

Harris: If you are telling me that I have no evidence that you have ever handled a gun, I think that's true, yes, I would go along with all three of you on that. I think that's right isn't it?

Matthews: I have handled guns, shotguns, you know. [Matthews had had a sporting-gun licence when he used to go pigeon shooting.]

Harris: No, but I mean been nicked with them.

Matthews: Anything like that is nothing at all to do with me.

Harris: No.

Matthews: You know, as long as you are gentleman enough to give us your word that it is straightforward . . .

Harris: It will be.

Matthews: Then I will make arrangements to come in legally represented.

Harris then warned Matthews that the leak in the *Evening Standard* was only the start of the publicity that was going to break over the next few days. Matthews said that he was annoyed that the police intervention had messed up their work schedule on the Greenwich site.

Harris: Yes, but that's been bending iron bars, hasn't it?

Matthews: Pardon.

Harris: I heard Frankie has been bending iron bars.

Matthews: Well, listen, cut that violent bit out will you? Cor dear, we are not violent men, you know that.

Harris: Well, there were aspects of the robbery, as I said I don't want you to admit anything on the telephone, but there were aspects of the robbery which appear to be violent. You may have an explanation for that when I see you.

Matthews: Yep. Let me tell you now I'm not waiting here much longer if it is connected with this killing at Braintree. I will give you my word I am straightforward and people must have told you. . . . I will make moves to come in legally represented and sort this out.

Harris: Well, where are you going to come?

Matthews: Well, I don't know yet, because I haven't contacted the other man.

Harris: As far as the murder is concerned we will take you to Braintree, but if you want me to meet you anywhere I will meet you and you can come with us.

Matthews: I can't speak for the other people, but wait until I see them and I will very likely contact you again.

Harris: Yes. The only thing that I would like to point out to you Chic is that the longer you delay it, the more difficult it is going to become for you because all the police officers in the Metropolitan area and the Essex area now are fully aware of this business . . . you are now being hounded and because of the involvement on a robbery where violence was used and because one of your very, very close associates is charged with murder . . . if you want I can come and meet you tonight, or I can meet you in the morning or do anything.

Matthews: I have got to contact the others first, you know what I mean, we have split up a bit.

Harris: Well, look stay out of the way for tonight, for Christ's sake, because you want to be brought in in reasonable circumstances.

Matthews: I don't want to be captured out, you know that. I want to come in and do it properly.

Harris: Well, you will take your chance I think is the saying that you used earlier on the other aspect, but we want to interview you.

Matthews: That is nothing to do with me either, guv'nor, I will point that out when we come in.

For a few more seconds Harris and Matthews discussed how they would contact each other again. According to the police, the coversation ended at 9.17 pm.

Matthews, naturally, was extremely concerned that his reason for being out of town – in fact his alibi – should be understood right from the start. But he knew that for anyone who lived outside the East End – and that included Harris – the Tibbs affair was not easy to understand. It was, as we have seen earlier, to do with codes of behaviour of people living in a tightly-knit community where violence was not uncommon. It concerned the influence that can be exerted by large cockney families, the feuds between them, vendettas harboured over many years perhaps because of a throwaway remark in a pub. But, above all, it concerned 'no narking' – the accepted rule that if you run into trouble you don't go home crying, and if it's trouble which involves the law you don't go crying to the police either.

A detailed look at the case of the Tibbs family is important to an understanding of the lives of the people written about in this book. The three wanted men, Molloy, Matthews and Sims, had all at one time or another worked for the Tibbses. George Ince had been friendly with them. None of the men wanted to appear as witnesses in the Tibbs trial: it could mean becoming too strongly identified with the Tibbs family.

At the time of the Tibbses' arrest, in the spring of 1972, the media talked of their 'terror rule' of the East End. The father, 'Big Jim' Tibbs, eventually dubbed 'the godfather', was cast as the autocratic manipulator of his three sons' criminal activities. It seemed an exaggerated picture to those who lived in the East End and had contact with the Tibbs family. Even though the Tibbses have now been convicted of very serious crimes, that sentiment still persists in some quarters.

The fact is that the violence in which the Tibbses became involved was limited to a very small circle of people.

The chain of events leading to their trial can be traced back to a feud between the Tibbses and another family called Nichols. The feud would not have seemed out of place in Shakespearian Verona and like most such feuds it had obscure, and apparently inconsequential, origins. It might even have started as a row within a family, for it is widely believed that the Tibbses and the Nicholses had been related at some distant time. The Tibbses were known through their scrap-metal business and the Nicholses through their interest in horse-breeding. Both had big tough sons who were keen on boxing.

The feud became important in the late sixties when Jimmy Tibbs junior was regarded as one of Britain's best middleweight boxing hopes. Jimmy had started making a reputation for himself as a schoolboy champion. He had boxed for West Ham Boys' Club and his ambition was to follow his clubmates Terry Spinks and Billy Walker and fight for the British championship. The Kray twins, who had had great respect for Big Jim and his large family for some time, spotted the potential of Jimmy junior and offered to manage his professional career. Big Jim was credited locally with an unusual degree of courage when he turned the offer down.

The Nicholses were less impressed with Jimmy's prospects. Over the Christmas of 1968 Albert Nichols, the eldest brother, was involved in an obscure bar-room argument about Jimmy's prowess with Jimmy's uncle, George 'Bogey' Tibbs. Some time later the same day Nichols ended up, beaten and suffering from a gunshot wound in Poplar Hospital. Both Jimmy Tibbs junior and his brother John were charged with the unlawful wounding of Nichols.

Police inquiries over the incident extended to Chic Matthews, who was then a partner with Big Jim, and also to Frankie Sims, who was then manager of the Star Café. On learning that he was wanted for questioning, Matthews went along of his own accord to Poplar police station where he was interviewed by CID officers and then taken to Poplar Hospital to be confronted by Nichols. Nichols said he did not know him and he was allowed to leave.

At the end of the trial Jimmy and John Tibbs were given two-year suspended sentences. The judge, Mr Justice Lyell, clearly indicated that he understood there were two sides to the argument. 'I sympathize with your feeling,' he said, in passing judgement, 'but at the same time, living in the part of London where you live, there is a great deal too much violence.' Matthews took note; his name had been mentioned throughout the trial and when it was over he had a serious discussion with Big Jim about his position in connection with the family. It was agreed that the Tibbs family had enemies and, because Matthews was a partner in the Tibbs firm, those enemies could also be his. Anxious not to be involved in any trouble of this kind he dissolved the partnership. Matthews felt that when it became known that he was no longer directly linked with the family those in dispute with the Tibbses would leave him alone. He was wrong.

Matthews opened a commercial truck business at Pier Head in North Woolwich. Although he had never had any formal training he had become a competent mechanic and made a reasonable living buying and selling lorries and vans. One day in 1970 two men paid him a visit. They demanded 'insurance' money which Matthews refused to pay. From that moment things went from bad to worse. Without the 'insurance' Matthews knew that his business might suffer. It was a constant threat. He refused to let his wife answer the telephone or let his children go out in the street on their own. The police called several times at his home to search it. According to his wife, when they found nothing they would go away saying they had received false information. The threats against Matthews continued, and the Tibbses became more deeply involved in violent incidents. There followed an alarming sequence of attacks.

In November 1970 Robert Tibbs, the youngest son, was viciously assaulted and badly cut up outside the Rose of Denmark pub in Canning Town. The wounds to his face and throat, one of which almost severed his jugular vein, required forty stitches. The incident was not reported to the police.

In January 1971 Ted Machin, a man of fifty who was reckoned to be a close friend of the Tibbses, and made it part of his business to know what was going on in the East End, was asleep in his bed in the downstairs front room of his house in Cecil Road, Forest Gate, when a shotgun was poked through the window and fired into the room. The main blast missed him by inches, but some pellets caught him in the groin. Two weeks later Ted Machin's nephew, Micky Machin, was approached by four men as he was sitting in his van about to drive off. They pointed a shotgun at the driver's seat window and fired it. The blast shattered all windows of the vehicle but by ducking under the dashboard he escaped unhurt.

On April 22, there was an explosion at the Star Café where Sims worked. It was badly damaged. Police said they thought it had been caused by a gas leak. Three days later Jimmy Tibbs, the young boxer, was about to take his four-year-old son from his home in Park Avenue, East Ham, to nursery school in his van. As he turned the ignition the engine blew up and pieces of the bonnet were blown forty feet up into the air. Some of the flying parts smashed through the window of a greengrocer's shop owned by Jimmy's uncle, just up the road. A Scotland Yard spokesman was quoted afterwards as saying: 'It looks like it was meant to be a frightener, but it nearly turned out to be a killer.' It was treated by the police as a case of attempted murder.

Next month, May, the attention of the Tibbses' enemies was turned once again on Matthews. He had several vehicles on display in the forecourt of his lorry front in North Woolwich. Handbrakes were mysteriously taken off and lorries ran into each other, causing considerable damage. Equipment, including spray plants, compressors and valuable spare parts were stolen. Matthews was making quite a lot of money at the time and he had a new Mercedes car. One night, when it was parked outside his home a lorry drove into it. The following day Matthews received phone-calls which referred to the so-called accident; it was suggested he would be better off paying the 'insurance money'.

In July, a bomb exploded by Big Jim's office at the scrap-metal yard. The office was empty, but a passer-by was knocked over by the blast. A detective was quoted as saying: 'This gang must be found before people are killed.' Late that summer a close friend of the Tibbses was sitting in his car when it was peppered with seven bullets. Remarkably he survived.

In September 1971, Matthews was coming home late from a greyhound meeting when he stopped for a meal at a Chinese restaurant. Three men approached him, accused him of being a friend of the Tibbses, and told him to warn them that they were in for a lot more trouble. He ignored the men and they went out. When he left the restaurant he was attacked and hit on the head with what he thought was a chopper. Blood was coming from the wound, but Matthews did not want the local police inquiring into the incident so he drove out of the area to a hospital in the West End where he was treated by the casualty officer. Matthews gave a false name and made some excuse about an accident. Thirty stitches were put in the wounds in his head. By Christmas 1971 Matthews had decided for his own and his family's sake to move away from home, but the attacks continued: one night his Mercedes was covered with paint stripper. On another night his premises at Pier Head were burned down.

In the early hours of April 4, 1972, more than 150 policemen, under the direction of Albert Wickstead, carried out a series of raids on fifty homes in East and South-East London. It was said to be an attempt to stop small-time gangs stepping into the void left by the Krays and the Richardsons, who had been jailed four years earlier. Twenty men were detained. Among the matters being investigated, reported the London *Evening News*, were the attacks against the scrap-metal dealer Jimmy Tibbs junior, who was about to make a comeback to professional boxing. More raids were carried out by the police on the following day – this time in daylight.

On April 5, 1972, at City Road police station – a discreet three miles from their homes – twelve men of the original twenty picked up were charged. Three were charged with attempted murder, eleven with conspiracy to cause grievous bodily harm and one with dishonestly receiving stolen property. It was, in fact, a round-up of the Tibbs family. Those accused of three cases of attempted murder included Jimmy Tibbs, the boxer, and Micky Machin. Eight others were accused of conspiracy to cause grievous bodily harm, including Big Jim Tibbs.

Even though these men had been charged, Matthews, Sims

and Molloy reckoned that the police would still be looking for witnesses. There were indications that those who had testified against the Tibbses would not turn up in court. When the twelve men were brought to court during the second week in April, Wickstead warned the magistrates that witnesses who would give evidence against the Tibbses were terrified: some refused to live at their home addresses. In those circumstances the police would reasonably still be on the lookout for any available evidence: the fact that Matthews, Sims and Molloy had been so closely associated with the Tibbs family made the reason they had given for being away from their homes when the police called on May 2 quite plausible.

Towards the end of September it looked as though there was going to be another trial in which the three men might be involved. Eight men, including some of the chief prosecution witnesses against the Tibbses, were charged with violent crimes, including attempted murder and grievous bodily harm. Those charges, it must be stressed, had nothing to do with the Tibbs trial. But after a week in custody several of the men were released on bail and on October 19 the Director of Public Prosecutions announced that the case would be dropped. Some witnesses were no longer available; others would 'possibly be reluctant to give evidence'. The eight men were each awarded £100 costs out of public funds.

But the trial of the Tibbses went ahead: it ended in January 1973, after forty-three days. Jimmy Tibbs, the boxer, was jailed for ten years, convicted of attempted murder, unlawful wounding, assaulting a police officer and possessing a firearm. John Tibbs received seven years for attempted murder. Robert Tibbs was given fifteen months on a charge of wounding, and the boy's father Big Jim Tibbs was given fifteen years for conspiracy to pervert the course of justice, conspiracy to blackmail and possessing ammunition.

When the Tibbs family was locked up it was not, however, the end of violence in the area. Immediately following the trial the front door window of Mrs Tibbs's home in East Ham was smashed; the circumstances were unexplained. She also received, she said, anonymous telephone threats. A petrol bomb was thrown at a lorry operated by the man who took over the

Tibbses' scrap yard. And then at the end of May, Micky Machin's uncle, Ted, was killed by the blast from a double-barrelled shotgun fired from a passing car as he walked along the street outside his home. Detective Chief Superintendent George Leslie of West Ham police suggested at the time that his death was the result of family feuding. It was a fair assumption. At fifty-two, Ted Machin had been around a long time in the East End. It was said he knew too much. At the same time Chic Matthews, too, continued to be a target: he received threatening letters.

Superintendent Harris's warning to Matthews that the *Evening Standard* report of December 6 was only the start of the publicity was no idle threat. On the following Sunday, December 10, on Independent Television's programme 'Police Five', the presenter, Shaw Taylor (known in the East End as 'Whispering Grass'), named the four men wanted in connection with inquiries into the Barn murder. They were Matthews, Molloy, Sims and one other man. Their photographs were flashed on the screen and released to the national newspapers.

The campaign had its intended result: Matthews, Molloy and Sims gave themselves up the next day. The fourth man was arrested five days later in a furnished house he had rented at Penrhyn Bay, near Llandudno in North Wales. On November 17 Essex police said he would not be charged with any offences relating to the murder.

Molloy was the first to be seen by the Essex police. Just after 1 o'clock on the afternoon of Monday December 11, three detectives met him at the offices of his solicitors in Walthamstow. They arrested him immediately in connection with the bullion robbery. He made no reply and was escorted by car to Braintree. Matthews and Sims gave themselves up together, having made previous arrangements with their solicitors in Commercial Road. From their offices they were taken to Leman Street police station. Both men were immediately arrested for the bullion robbery and taken separately to Braintree. Matthews refused to say anything in the car, but according to the police Sims answered some questions.

Sims was asked specifically where he was on the night of November 4. He said he was in a pub in Sittingbourne with Matthews and Molloy and that George Ince had gone to London. Ince had left after they had all been to a sauna bath and hadn't been seen again until Sunday lunchtime. According to Detective Constable David Delamain, Sims said that he wished he had given himself up when he and Matthews had seen the police outside R & N Motors that rainy Monday afternoon – it would have avoided all the publicity in the papers.

'Why didn't you?' asked one of the policemen.

'Well, I couldn't just do it then could I?' said Sims. 'I have to make arrangements first.'

'If you want to keep on running you've got to expect us to catch you any way we can,' said the officer.

'Yes, I suppose so,' said Sims, 'but putting it in the papers like that . . . no matter what the result is no one will believe it now, will they? You know what the papers are.'

7 · The trials of George Ince

> '*You may have a feeling of deep unease. There is something funny about the whole affair*' – Victor Durand QC, for Ince, in his closing speech at the second Barn murder trial.

The Crown Court building in Chelmsford, an Essex town of great ordinariness, dominates the central square on which it stands. It is a huge and ornate construction, set well back from the main road and approached up shallow steps. Inside, one might be in any court in the country. Chelmsford was not accustomed to showpiece trials, but for the month of May 1973 it was under the spotlight. In the six months since the murder the names of Robert Patience, whose restaurant and motel lay only a dozen or so miles from the courthouse, and George Ince, the man from the East End of whom little was known, had become familiar to everybody. Considerable precautions were taken by the police, who wanted no violent incidents, no attempts to free their prisoner, to mar the trial. Each day Ince arrived at the court from Brixton prison in a black maria escorted by police cars.

The public gallery was always packed – mostly with little old ladies who leaned eagerly forward trying to catch a glimpse of the accused – and there were queues outside the courthouse each morning before the court sat. Everybody wanted to come and stare at the man who was widely assumed to have committed the murder. Those who had followed the case rather more closely might have remarked that there was only one man in the dock whereas two men had been involved in the shooting.

Each afternoon at four there would be a rush of news reporters making for the line of telephone boxes just across the road from the courthouse. The staff of the Saracen's Head, the pub by the court building, did business as they never had before, serving drinks to lawyers and journalists, laying on teas for reporters, taking messages from anxious newspaper offices. Chelmsford, usually a dreamy and unexciting town, enjoyed its month of national attention.

During the first few days of the trial the Ince family became well known to the public. There was his mother Minnie, an old lady of eighty who moved slowly. Throughout the proceedings she retained an aura of dignity and composure, and she was usually allowed to sit in the main court-room rather than having to go up to the public gallery. Ince's five sisters showed none of her restraint. They were there to stand by their brother, to tell the world he was innocent and to make public their feelings about the Essex police. Their outspokenness became a feature of all the trials in which Ince was to take part. They chattered with the press, their abusive comments about the police diluted only by the cockney wit with which they were delivered. They made loud comments when they were sitting upstairs in the public gallery and frequently had to be silenced. The police grew to dislike them intensely. They tended to look straight ahead and walk quickly past whenever they found themselves in the immediate vicinity of one of the Ince family.

The trial opened on May 2. Ince was charged with murdering Muriel Patience, attempting to murder Robert and Beverley Patience, wounding Robert and Beverley Patience, and stealing about £900 in cash and cheques from Robert Patience. He pleaded not guilty to all charges. The judge was Mr Justice Melford Stevenson, whose trials over recent years have attracted much publicity.

He was nearly seventy at the time and had a well-earned reputation for harsh sentencing. His famous trials include the Garden House affair in Cambridge, when he sentenced six students to prison terms of up to eighteen months for their part in a violent demonstration against the Greek regime, and the trial of the Kray twins and their accomplices, when he doled out sentences totalling 142 years – a British record. His punishments, particularly for the first offender, have been strongly criticized: he once sent a nineteen-year-old youth to

Borstal for robbery with the hope that 'no soft-hearted official will recommend your early release'. His courtroom style is prickly and donnish, and when passing sentence his speeches often have the severity and withering contempt of a headmaster admonishing a small boy. As a prosecution QC he used the technique of the instant pause before cross-examination which tends to bring a shaky witness out in a cold sweat. He indicates impatience with a witness – or counsel – simply by a change in facial expression. Though he will appear on occasion to be taking no interest whatever in the proceedings his incisive mind is constantly alert, and does not suffer muddled argument lightly.

He has been involved in several murder trials: he was part of the prosecution team in the case in which Dr Bodkin Adams was acquitted and he defended Ruth Ellis, the last woman to be hanged in Britain. As a judge he was once criticized in the Appeal Court for failing to put before a jury, which convicted a man of murder, a pathologist's theory that the man could have been killed in self-defence. The omission, said Lord Justice Edmund Davies, was a fatal flaw, making the guilty verdict unsafe. Off duty his friends think of him as warm-hearted and applaud his ready wit.

Two days before the trial began Ince's solicitors made an application to have it transferred to another judge. The application was made in chambers, so the grounds on which it was made were never revealed. In any case, Melford Stevenson turned down the application. Ince's legal advisers were furious. After the trial an editorial in the *Guardian* remarked:

> No one with experience of criminal courts can doubt that some judges have earned a reputation for being prosecution-minded, for interventions and comments which can harry the defence. In one or two extreme cases the Appeal Court has set aside verdicts on the ground of excessive intervention from the bench, but these are rare exceptions. More generally the question is one of court-room atmosphere – and it is by no means clear that an impatient judge actually assists the prosecution. A clever defence counsel can secure the sympathy of the jury

against such interventions and so bias their judgement in favour of the defence. What is clear is that a judge who fails to maintain judicial detachment does not help to ensure that justice is done.

It was chance that Melford Stevenson was given the trial, in that he was on that judges' circuit at the time. But it might have been better if there had been a special selection for a trial which was bound to be controversial. In the event, the fact that Melford Stevenson was chosen contributed to some of the sensational outbursts from the dock which were to follow.

The prosecutor, as in the trials of all the alleged Barn murderers, was John Leonard QC, a kindly and gentle man whose wife, unfailingly attentive, sat at the back of the court. She travels with him to all his trials, taking a personal interest, and, as she says, looking after him. Leonard is said to have felt deeply upset when it emerged that Ince had been wrongfully charged, and to have communicated this feeling to him. During Ince's two trials for the Barn murder Leonard prosecuted with all the articulate conviction expected of the representative of the Crown. Ince was defended by Victor Durand QC, a more extrovert and theatrical counsel than Leonard. From the start he believed sincerely in Ince's innocence, and the constant friction between him and the judge was only too apparent. His task was formidable: Beverley Patience had positively identified his client as the murderer.

The chief prosecution witnesses were Bob and Beverley Patience. Throughout the trial Bob Patience found it hard to resist making gratuitous remarks in answer to no question at all, and seldom missed an opportunity of telling the court that the man sitting in the dock was the one who killed his wife. Ince's temper gave out early on. Soon after Bob Patience began his evidence came the first of Ince's many outbursts. Patience made one of his direct accusations and Ince, who had been sitting quietly, leapt to his feet and shouted at him: 'You know I was not the one who did it. Why don't you tell the truth?' Patience replied, 'I am.' The judge scowled, and the prison officers pulled Ince back into his seat. He later apologized to the court.

From the beginning the strain showed on Ince's face. He sat in the dock leaning forward slightly, his face a study in concentration. He shook his head in disbelief from time to time, and the veins on his forehead bulged more as the trial progressed. He said later that his feeling of despair grew daily. It was impossible for him to describe the feeling of being tried for a murder he knew he had not committed. Yet hearing the evidence against him piling up day by day, he began to believe he would be convicted.

Patience was rigorously questioned by Durand about the fact that he had not at first picked Ince out on the identification parade. He admitted that he had walked behind the line of men on the parade but, he said, it was not until he had had the chance to study Ince from behind for some ten minutes in the magistrates court, two weeks later, that he became certain that Ince was the gunman who had been in his house that night. Patience also said that his son David had remembered seeing Ince at a party of his in Jersey some five years before. But when David Patience came to give evidence he said that yes, he had thought that at first, but he was now convinced that he was wrong about it. (In fact, Ince has never been to Jersey.)

Beverley was the Crown's most important witness, and from the Crown's point of view she was a good one. She had been in the front room at the Sun Lido House throughout the confrontation with the gunman, and unlike her father she had positively and immediately picked Ince out on the identification parade. Her words carried more conviction because she was nervous and tentative in court, and because the jury knew that she had been literally within a fraction of an inch of her life. On the third day of the trial she broke down and wept in the witness-box. She had been provoked by another of Ince's outbursts. She was being questioned on the important matter of the photographs she had been shown of Ince before the ID parades. She agreed with Durand that she had been shown a photograph of Ince just seventy-two hours before she had picked him out on the identification parade at Colchester police station. Ince stood up in the dock and staring angrily at Beverley, he yelled: 'Why don't you tell the truth?' Beverley, who had been sitting in the witness-box because of her frail condition, bent forward and covered her face with her hands and murmured: 'No, no.' She then started sobbing. One of Ince's sisters shouted from the gallery: 'No, George, no.'

Melford Stevenson looked enraged. 'I had better make notes on that outburst,' he said coldly and adjourned the court for twenty minutes. When Ince was brought back into the dock he said to the judge: 'I'd like to apologize to the court, sir, but I'm not the man who did it.' Melford Stevenson snapped: 'Keep quiet,' and announced that he was going to hear the rest of Beverley's evidence in Ince's absence. He was not going to risk any more outbursts of the kind he had suffered twice in this very important trial. Ince was taken downstairs to the cells and Beverley completed her evidence. As the next witness, her brother David, was going into the box the judge declared: 'If the defendant can restrain himself he can be brought back.' Ince returned to the dock.

During the weekend recess which fell halfway through this first trial, Ince's relatives sent a telegram to the then Lord Chancellor, Lord Hailsham, alleging irregularities in the conduct of the case. They still objected to the choice of judge for the trial.

The first few days of the trial had been sufficient to earn it that overworked newspaper description of sensational. But the events that followed were, in fact, even more so. The tension continued to increase and it reached crisis point on the fifth day of the trial.

By that stage Ince was sure that he was going to be convicted. In what appeared to be a hopeless final gesture of defiance he decided to turn on the judge. His move came after a long conference with Durand and his junior counsel Robert Flach, during which Ince had told them categorically that he wanted a different judge. He said he believed he was not getting a fair trial; it had to be stopped for if he was convicted he would go to prison for life.

Durand told him that it was impossible to change the judge;

Ince retorted that if that was the case his only option was to sack his counsel. There were things he was determined to say to the judge which his advocates could not say on his behalf. He had the right to defend himself and if that was the only way to get what he wanted then that was what he was going to do. Ince had become convinced of the necessity of this extreme action after a visit from an old friend who perusaded him that this course was the only one which could save him. He is now certain that it actually did.

Durand addressed the judge. Ince, he said, wanted to make a statement which his counsel could not, with propriety, make on his behalf. They had attempted to dissuade him from the course on which he was about to embark but Ince had told him that he wanted his defence counsel to take no further part in representing him, and that being his client's expressed wish it was Durand's duty to comply with it.

Ince himself had no truck with the niceties of court etiquette and if the relationship between defendant and judge was already strained what he had to say next destroyed it beyond repair. Ince had clearly thought carefully about what he was going to say. His statement was calm and controlled, not the kind of hysterical outburst he had made earlier. Looking straight at Melford Stevenson he said: 'I am an Englishman, born and bred in England, and I want an English trial. I do not want Mr Durand or Mr Flach to represent me any more while you are sitting on the bench. I am completely innocent of the charges and knew nothing whatsoever about it.'

Melford Stevenson was equally controlled in reply. 'I can only tell you,' he said, 'that I fear you are being unwise.'

Ince retorted: 'You have been nothing else but rude. I would like Mr Durand to defend me in any other court before any other judge but you, sir.'

Ince was not of course entitled to choose his judge, said Melford Stevenson. He could not permit any defendant such a right. There was a right of challenge to jurors but no right of challenge to a judge. It was an application he simply could not grant. Ince then tried to leave the dock and go down to the cells but the judge ordered him to sit down. In the hushed court-room, Flach went across to the dock and whispered with his client. A message was conveyed to Durand, who told Melford Stevenson that Ince wanted to take no further part in the trial. He wished to go down to the cells and stay there. The judge refused to allow it: Ince must remain in the dock. Ince's temper flared again and he shouted at the bench: 'I do not want this case to be heard in front of you. You are biased, rude, everything.' He struggled with the prison officers in an attempt to leave the dock. 'Keep him there,' yelled the judge.

Durand said to the bench in a calm voice: 'As I understand the position from my client, my lord, he expresses absolutely no criticism at the action of his solicitors, Mr Flach and myself. But he desires that his counsel take no further part from this point and it is therefore my duty to comply.'

Melford Stevenson's reaction to this was to decide that the trial should proceed without Ince's defence. He told the prosecution to continue calling witnesses. The defendant would remain in the dock and it was up to him to question the witnesses if he wanted to. The trial continued, after a fashion. It was a bizarre affair: Durand and Flach remained sitting in the court but played no further part. Ince himself stood in the dock, leaning on the rail, his back to the judge, interrupting occasionally as Leonard continued to examine his witnesses. Ince went particularly for Chief Inspector Gorham, who had organized the identity parade in Colchester where Ince was picked out by Beverley and David, but not by Bob Patience. He accused Gorham of placing him third in the line on the parade because he was third on the card of pictures shown to Beverley by the police. The accusation was ignored.

The next day of the trial, Wednesday May 9, was the last. Since Ince had sacked his counsel no defence evidence was offered, so after Leonard had completed the prosecution case it only remained for the judge to sum up. But Ince had not finished. He produced yet another dramatic diversion at the beginning of the day when, to the astonishment of all, he asked to be given the truth drug. He held up a newspaper containing an account of how the drug had been given to a sixteen-year-old boy during a murder trial in the United States. If the boy could have it, asked Ince, why couldn't he? If necessary, he would happily pay for it. Melford Stevenson, for the first time appearing a little ruffled, simply said that the drug could not be supplied and, in an effort to restore the usual legal dignity to the court, asked Ince if he would like to reinstate his defence counsel. Ince replied flatly, no, and repeated that he thought the judge biased and rude.

Ince interrupted no less than sixteen times during the summing up, but Melford Stevenson carried on, unheeding. The jury would have a difficult job, he said, because there was no defence evidence. Ince had been offered the chance of calling evidence on his own behalf but he had rejected it. 'He alone knows why he rejected it, and it would be wrong of us to speculate. In a case of this kind we must not speculate about anything,' he declared. Ince had the right to say nothing. The major question facing the jury was that of identity, the judge said, and evidence of identification always presented many hazards. The prophetic significance of that statement was lost in the welter of words which made up the judge's closing address.

Melford Stevenson concentrated, predictably, on the identification evidence of Beverley Patience, and emphasized her composure in the witness-box. It was clear that he wanted her evidence to be taken seriously by the jury. He told the jury not to allow themselves to be prejudiced against Ince by anything he had said or done or not done. They were to make up their minds on the evidence alone. But, he said, it would not have escaped the jury that 'this case had taken a course which is, happily, unusual. It won't have escaped you that the behaviour of the defendant has from time to time been such as may have surprised you.' Judges usually explain 'reasonable doubt' to a jury when stressing that their agreed verdict must be beyond 'reasonable doubt'. Melford Stevenson warned the jury against interpreting reasonable doubt as 'some fanciful doubt which people might entertain who wanted to avoid a difficult decision'.

The jury went out just before 3 o'clock in the afternoon. They came back twice for guidance; it was the lack of any defence evidence which was troubling them. Melford Stevenson told them that the absence of a defence was Ince's own choice and his own right. Ince retorted from the dock: 'But I objected to you, sir, not to the jury.'

When, by early evening, the jury had been unable to reach a unanimous verdict, the judge considered it necessary to recall them. The law says that all twelve members of a jury must agree on their verdict. But the judge has the right to advise them that he will accept a majority verdict – that is no more than two dissenters – if in his judgement the jury has been out so long that the reaching of a unanimous verdict seems impossible. That is what Melford Stevenson did in this case. When the jury had failed to agree on a majority verdict, he advised them that, if necessary, it was possible for them to come to a decision that the defendant was guilty, not of murder, but of manslaughter.

Although it was late the court was still packed when the jury finally returned at 9.30 pm ready to deliver their verdict. Ince's family was nervous and tense, hoping, without much conviction, that because the jury had been out so long it was more likely that they had disagreed and would therefore acquit. Ince was brought up from the cells, the strain showing clearly on his face. He sat down without saying anything. Then he stood to hear the verdicts. The jury foreman said that they had been unable to agree on a verdict in any of the six charges.

A cheer went up from the gallery. The judge dismissed the jury and immediately ordered a retrial. They had tried their best, he said, but agreement had eluded them. He had no alternative but to order another trial, even though that was a profound public misfortune and a profound private misfortune for everyone involved.

Ince insisted on having the final say. As the prison officers tried to lead him back downstairs he looked back at the jury and said: 'I would like to thank the members of the jury for giving me the chance to state my case and let my case go forward in front of a truthful judge.' He turned to Melford Stevenson for the last time and said unemotionally: 'You have been biased.' The judge smiled and left the court.

So it was back to square one, and only a weekend elapsed before Ince was again in Chelmsford Crown Court. The case was the same, with two significant differences. The judge this time was Mr Justice Eveleigh, less famous than his predecessor; and this time the key defence witness, Ince's alibi, appeared. Ince's solicitor, now Ralph Haeems, had applied for a postponement until he had had a chance to see the transcript of the first trial. He said it was unfair that the second trial should start so soon after the completion of the first. But his application was turned down.

The one piece of forensic evidence offered by the prosecution was dropped for this trial. The police had found turquoise blue acrylic fibres on a blue overcoat belonging to Ince that they had taken from his sister Rose's home. They had established that these fibres were similar to those in the covering of the settee in Sun Lido House. It seemed far-fetched because Beverley had been quite certain that the gunman was wearing a beige raincoat. And Rose knew that Ince's coat had been in her house for about ten months.

Then, soon after her brother had told her about the fibres, she was brushing a stool at home when she noticed some blue acrylic fibres. Was that where those on the coat had come from? She had just sold a three-piece suite covered in the same cloth.

Ince's solicitor decided that a top forensic scientist, Dr Julius Grant, should be called in. He compared a sample of the fibres supplied by the police with those which Rose had collected. And he examined the suite Rose had sold. The fibres were similar, he decided. The police withdrew this part of the prosecution case for the retrial, which opened on May 14.

John Leonard rose to his feet to deliver the case for the Crown yet again. He was beginning to know it all by heart. There was no pretence to the new jury that the case had not been heard before. Leonard remarked with typical legal understatement: 'It would be unrealistic to pretend that this is not a retrial, there having been a previous trial in which the jury disagreed. Normally the jury does not know there is a retrial, but in this case, and because of the countrywide publicity given to the first trial, it would be totally unrealistic to pretend it had not happened.' He suggested, hopefully, that the jury might put out of its mind all it had heard and read about the case.

It was like an action replay as Bob Patience strode into court quite prepared and often eager to tell his story again. He seemed more confident than before and hardly had his questioning begun when he pointed to Ince and declared assuredly: 'The man in the dock shot my wife.' At best, Patience could not be considered an ideal witness, and on many occasions Leonard must have wished that his second most important witness would stick to answering the questions.

On the second day of the trial the atmosphere became heated as Victor Durand, once again able to defend his client, cross-examined. Patience decided to introduce a new element into the trial: he said that on the identification parade for Ince he had asked those taking part to say the words: 'I want the keys to the safe.' One of the men, he said, had clearly not used his natural voice when he said it. This was fresh evidence, remarked Durand. Why hadn't he mentioned it at the first trial? 'You didn't ask me,' said Patience. 'I was waiting for an opportunity to say yesterday why I know that that man over there [he pointed at Ince] shot myself, my wife and my daughter. This question has never been put to me in this court, in the magistrates court or in the "do-it-yourself" trial last week.'

It was typical Bob Patience. It was true that on the identification parade, on which he had picked out the wrong man, Patience had asked those taking part to say: 'I want the keys to the safe.' This was recorded in Gorham's account of the parade, again in Patience's statement after the parade when he said he should have picked out Ince, and yet again in Patience's deposition at the committal. But there was no mention at all of one of the men not using his natural voice. Durand snapped: 'You keep your place as a witness of fact.' 'I lost my wife,' was Patience's reply. The judge intervened: 'Don't quarrel with Mr Durand,' he told him. He knew it must be distressing for him, but it was in everyone's interest if he just answered the questions to speed things up.

Durand made much of the fact that Bob Patience had not picked out Ince on the identity parade. He dwelt on David Patience's identification, based on a brief glimpse of the men leaving the Barn in a car, and his later retracted statement about having met Ince in Jersey five years earlier. Ince had never been to Jersey. But instead of just leaving it that he had made a mistake he added to the confusion by saying that by some extraordinary coincidence he had been muddling up the George Ince in the dock with another man he had met who not only bore the same name but also looked rather similar. The judge remarked sceptically that this seemed a remarkably long shot on David Patience's part. Durand also questioned rigorously on the matter of the change of shirt during the identification parade, a point on which Bob Patience's second-thoughts identification, itself rather worrying, depended.

As soon as Durand began Ince's defence it became clear that it would hang on his alibi, the woman, who was to remain a mystery to the jury and the public until the trial was over. Before she was called, Ince himself went into the witness-box, where he showed none of the anger of his dock outbursts but answered the questions calmly and quietly. 'I am completely innocent,' he said. He told Durand that he had spent the night of the murder with a Mrs Doris Grey and that he was in love with her. Rather than telling the court her address he was allowed to write it on a piece of paper which was passed to the jury. Leonard made a strenuous effort to make Ince reveal her real identity to the jury. What, he asked him, was her real name? Durand interrupted: it was Grey, he said. Eveleigh directed Ince to answer the question but Durand said there was a danger of introducing material which had no bearing on Ince's guilt or innocence.

The jury was sent out, and there followed a lengthy debate between Durand, Leonard and the judge about whether the jury should be told that Mrs Grey was in fact the wife of Charlie Kray. It was finally agreed that the jury would be told only that Grey was not the name she had always had. Ince described how he had been with her on the night of the murder and had left on the Sunday morning to return to the Whitstable caravan site.

Some of the jury must have had a good idea of who Mrs Grey really was; those members who didn't must have been thoroughly confused. By the end of the trial they knew that her husband was 'away'. There were constant warnings about guilt by association, talk of brothers-in-law who used to run a billiard hall, and once Leonard accidentally let slip the word

Kray in front of the jury. But for those jurymen who were not well informed about East End life and famous past trials there was a problem. Here was this mystery married woman, the major plank in the defence of the man whose guilt or innocence they had to determine, and they were allowed to know no more than that she slept with Ince on the key night, and that he was in love with her.

The jury was to see the woman herself in the witness-box. It had been a traumatic decision for all concerned. Durand realized that it was essential that she should appear as long as her true identity was not revealed. Juries are only human and he knew that if the jury were aware that his key witness was the wife of a Kray they might well be less inclined to take her seriously. Mrs Grey was guilty of no crime, but in the public eye the name Kray was synonymous with violence and gangland. To a public with just a passing knowledge of their activities a Kray was a Kray, the name was enough. But it was a risk Ince had to take: Durand decided she should testify.

Ince was always reluctant for Mrs Grey to appear. He believed, perhaps naïvely, that her original statement would have been sufficient to prevent him ever being charged with the murder, and he was reluctant to have his private life bandied about a court of law and, from there, all over the newspapers. Most of all, he was worried about Mrs Grey herself. He loved her: that he had persisted with the relationship for so long in the face of the obvious possible repercussions was an indication of his depth of feeling. He knew that a court appearance would be a painful and frightening experience for her, and would almost certainly bring to an end any pretence that her marriage could survive.

Mrs Grey herself did not imagine when she made her statement that it would result in her appearance in the witness-box, but she had always been prepared to tell the truth on Ince's behalf. When it became clear that she would have to give evidence she went to Maidstone prison to tell her husband Charlie. It seems that while he must have been aware of the fact that there was some relationship between Ince and his wife, Kray did not know until that moment the seriousness of the relationship, or that his wife and Ince were sleeping together. He said later that it came as a terrible shock to him, like a punch in the stomach. But according to Mrs Grey, while he was angry and hurt he still agreed that it was right for her to give evidence. She could not let an innocent man be convicted of murder. She saw Kray again a couple of weeks after the trial, and found him cold and detached but not critical of her having given evidence.

Mrs Grey was in an extremely tense and nervous state when she arrived at the court to be called as Mrs Doris Grey. She was visibly shaking at times and often her voice sank to a whisper; she had to be told to speak up. When Leonard was cross-examining her she nearly burst into tears. She is a Roman Catholic and she crossed herself after taking the oath. The court was silent, the atmosphere heavy, as she gave evidence. There were, of course, those in the court – some members of the jury, and some in the public gallery – who did not know who she really was.

She said she had changed her name by deed poll. She said that as far as she knew her husband did not know of her relationship with Ince, but she was in love with him and had spent the night of the murder in bed with him. Leonard, inevitably, suggested that she was making it all up to provide an alibi for the man she loved, but she insisted she was telling the absolute truth. Close to tears, she said that Ince had never left her side the whole night. 'I would like you to bear in mind the publicity I am getting. I stand to lose my home and my family. I am a Catholic and I would not come here to lie.'

In his summing-up Durand spoke of the public degradation Mrs Grey had suffered by confessing her adultery in a public court, arguing that she had given a heartfelt answer to Ince's plea for the truth to be revealed. He talked of Mrs Grey's husband as a man not free to interfere with the relationship she was having with Ince. He could not even roam the streets, but that day might come.

In the end the case rested, as it had throughout, on identification. Durand talked about it; so did the judge. Durand recalled that some of the most spectacular miscarriages of justice had been brought about by wrong identification of the accused. In this case the witnesses had seen photographs of the accused: was there not a risk that Ince's face had been made unintentionally familiar to the person who was afterwards to be called as a witness?

On the penultimate day of the trial there was another surprise development: the judge ordered a police guard to be put on all the members of the jury. He announced he had heard that a juryman believed that he had been followed when he went home the previous night, so he had arranged for police officers to keep each jury member under surveillance for the rest of the trial. The jurymen were not to talk to the policemen. At the end of the day's hearing each juryman left the court in the company of two plain-clothes policemen, and detectives kept a watch on their houses throughout the night. The Ince family was enraged. It made it look, they felt, as though somebody was trying to threaten the jury into acquitting their George. It was bound to prejudice them against him.

May 23, almost seven months after the murder, was the day on which the jury had to decide whether or not George Ince was the murderer. The queue outside the courthouse was the longest yet and extra police were on duty inside. No one was surprised when the unexpected happened yet again. Even before the day's proceedings had started word filtered out about the arrival of a mysterious letter. It was addressed to Durand at the court and it had arrived that morning, postmarked the previous day in Wisbech, Cambridgeshire. It was signed with a single capital T. It began: 'The defendant Mr Ince did not commit the murder. I did. It was my idea. I had two helpers. I'd be willing to declare myself if you, Mr Durand, could guarantee that the two who helped, or rather took part in it, were not prosecuted.'

T went on to say that he resembled Ince fairly closely and would give himself up 'quick' if it was agreed his two friends would not be prosecuted. The letter was given to the police but the jury, of course, were not told about it. The police sent it away for scientific analysis. Nothing more was heard about it. Later, when Nicholas de Clare Johnson was arrested for the murder, some wondered whether the 'declare myself' in T's letter was an obscure reference to Johnson. It will never be known.

Mr Justice Eveleigh summed up. He accepted that the jury would probably be speculating about who Mrs Grey was and he warned them against such speculation. It did not matter who her husband was, where he was, or what he had done. If Mrs Grey herself had a bad character reference the jury would have heard about it. Whatever a husband had done it didn't mean that the wife's lover was in contact with the husband or even knew him, or was in any way associated with what that man might have done. It was, necessarily, a circumlocutory way of warning the jury not to be prejudiced by the fact that Ince's lover was the wife of a Kray.

The jury retired and were out for more than three hours.

Ince's mother and his sister Betty waited outside the court when the verdicts were delivered. They couldn't bear to go inside. Six times the jury foreman said 'Not guilty', but after the first, for the murder, his voice was drowned by wild clapping and shouting in the public gallery. The voices of Ince's sisters, almost hysterical, rose high-pitched above the rest of the bedlam and the judge called for order and threatened to clear the court. The detectives who had been involved in the case sat on the police benches, staring straight ahead, their faces tight and expressionless. A spine-chilling scream came from the foyer, where Ince's sister Betty had been told, mistakenly, that her brother had been found guilty.

Ince himself looked more angry than pleased or relieved. He jumped to his feet and lunged across the dock, yelling 'It's your turn now.' He was dragged towards the steps to the cells as the din in the court reached a crescendo, and pushed down still yelling and swearing about money and corruption.

The court foyer was crowded with people, all jostling and pushing. Ince's relatives were grabbing reporters and calling for investigations. That was not the end of the matter, they said. The detectives remained inside the court. Uniformed policemen cleared the foyer, physically bundling some people out of the main entrance. A huge crowd built up on the courthouse steps. Eventually a path was cleared and the detectives emerged in a single column, tense and unsmiling, refusing to answer questions, as some members of the crowd jeered and hurled insults. Len White and his team were convinced that a murderer had been acquitted. Ince was taken back to Brixton prison to await trial for the Mountnessing bullion robbery. The case of the Barn murder was technically still open, although at that stage few imagined anybody else would ever be brought to trial. How could anyone else be tried for the murder when Beverley had said repeatedly that she was a hundred per cent certain George Ince was the man?

At the Barn that night the atmosphere was flat. A band played to the vast empty dining room. The police guard on the building was maintained, as it had been since the murder, by a police car out in the car park. In the bar David and Beverley Patience stood together, a rather forlorn pair, sipping nervously on their drinks and refusing to discuss the case with reporters. Their father spent the evening in the Sun Lido House. At about 11 o'clock he appeared in his bar chatting to a friend. He smiled and looked relaxed. He had several drinks and by 1 am he was seated at a table with reporters, chatting amiably. But he refused to discuss Ince or to comment on the verdict.

Three weeks later he was in the same bar when he had a visit from an Essex detective carrying a large brown box. He was returning the trial exhibits. Patience was horrified. There were his wife's blood-stained clothes and even the pink velvet cushion through which the shots had been fired. He knew that if Beverley was to see them she would become hysterical. He didn't want them, he told the policeman.

That night Patience took the macabre package out of the back door and crossed the yard to the caravan site behind the Barn. He went up to one of the huge waste-bins, leaned a ladder against it, and clambered up. When he was high enough to reach the top he pushed the package over the lip and into the bin. The next day the dustmen came and emptied it.

8 · The confession

'*This case does not in any sense depend on identification.*' – John Leonard QC, opening for the prosecution in the third Barn murder trial of John Brook and Nicholas de Clare Johnson.

THE commuter train from Chelmsford carrying John Brook and Nicholas de Clare Johnson arrived at Liverpool Street station during the morning of Guy Fawkes Day, 1972. The two men were tired and wet from their night wandering aimlessly through the Essex countryside. They had not seen a single policeman. Although back at Braintree a murder hunt was under way the killer and his accomplice felt confident that they were outside any net the police might cast, at least on that morning, eight hours after the shootings. Brook was convinced that the three people who had seen him with a gun in his hand were all dead. He had not even bothered to dispose of the Beretta automatic with which he had shot them; it was there in his pocket.

It was a Sunday morning and there were few people around. Brook took off his raincoat and shoved it into a left-luggage locker. The two men parted. The next time they were to meet they would be sitting side by side in the dock at Braintree.

Johnson crossed London to Waterloo station and from there he caught a train to Romsey in Hampshire, where he spent the day with Stanley Vane, the friend he had told the prison authorities he would be visiting when he left Pentonville the previous Friday night. During that day, already remorseful about the events of the previous night, he put his share of the stolen money in a dustbin and burnt it. That night he returned to London. He checked in at Pentonville on time at 10 pm. He was to remain in prison, working on the hostel scheme, until the following January.

Brook, on the other hand, was a free man. Three weeks before the murder he had completed the sentence resulting from a violent assault, and after he left Johnson at Liverpool Street he returned to his north London digs. He had been in lodgings in Hornsey Lane since October 27, little more than a week before the murder.

The following day he caught a train to Leeds to visit his grandmother, Mrs Barbara Senior. He did not go there often and she was surprised to see him. He stayed with her for a week and then returned to London. He still had the gun, but it didn't worry him because by then he knew that the police were on a completely different trail. The Barn murder was receiving widespread coverage in the press, and everything he read must have made him increasingly certain that he was a long way away from the wanted list.

On November 27 George Ince gave himself up and was charged with the murder. Brook knew that he was off the hook; once the police had a murder suspect in custody they didn't continue looking for someone else who might have committed the same murder. Brook relaxed. Unlike Johnson he did not spend his time worrying about what he had done; he was of a different temperament. He thought he had got away with murder, literally, and he began to live a relatively normal life.

The new year arrived and George Ince was in custody, awaiting trial. In the spring Brook moved north. He camped in the Lake District for two days, and then went into the local employment office for a job. There was a vacancy for a kitchen porter at the Salutation Hotel in Ambleside, and on March 29, a rucksack on his back, he arrived at the hotel and was taken on. He was given a bedroom which he had to share with two other men. Brook was working at the Salutation when the first trial of George Ince started in Chelmsford on May 2.

One of the men with whom Brook shared the bedroom was a petty criminal called Peter Hanson. He had moved in on April 23. Two days later he was playing round with a water pistol when Brook walked into the room. 'That's not much of a gun,' he said, and pulled his own Beretta out of the waistband of his trousers. Brook was very proud of his gun. He carried it in his waistband during the day and at night he hid it in a slit in his mattress. He made no great effort to prevent the gun being seen by other people at the hotel. On one occasion it was lying on the dressing-table when a maid, Barbara Graves, went into the room to tidy up. She picked it up and put it away in a drawer. While he was staying in Hornsey he had shown the gun to another lodger, a man called Hamilton.

Brook was only too keen to show Hanson how the gun worked. He also showed it to another employee at the Salutation, a man called Terence Holmes. Hanson said later that he had discussed the Barn murder trial with Brook. Brook had told him Ince had nothing to worry about: he would not be convicted of the murder because he hadn't done it. Brook claimed it was he, Brook, who had murdered Mrs Patience. He had gone to the Barn with his brother, but his brother had been scared to shoot, so he had fired the gun. Brook told Hanson that the gun he had shown him was the one he had used at the Barn, but when he showed the gun to Holmes he told him he had it to frighten the manager of the Salutation.

Hanson described an incident one night when Brook had been annoyed and had brandished the gun again. He had entered a room in which two members of the staff, a man called Trevor Mercer, the hotel's second chef, and his girl-friend, a chamber-maid, were watching television. Brook, according to Hanson, was annoyed about their relationship and had become very worked up about it. He ripped the television lead out of the wall and hurled at the door a chicken leg which he had been chewing. Then Brook came back and told Hanson he was going to get Trevor. He took out his gun, loaded it with one bullet, and left the room. Hanson heard a shot, and then Brook returned to the room.

Holmes also remembered the incident. It happened late at night on May 21 and Brook told him he was going to use the gun to frighten Trevor. Holmes heard a shot and then Brook came running back into the room where Holmes was waiting. He hid the gun under the wardrobe and said to Holmes: 'We don't know anything about it. It wasn't us.' It emerged that the shot had been fired out of the window.

For a murderer Brook was far from cautious. He continued to carry the murder weapon around with him, bragged about it, continued to flaunt it, even threatened to use it to frighten somebody. Between the murder of Mrs Patience and Brook's arrest at least four people had seen the gun – Hanson, Miss Graves, Holmes and Hamilton. Brook kept it in the rather obvious hiding-place he had made in the slit in his mattress.

Brook stayed at the Salutation until May 22, the day before the second trial ended in Ince's acquittal. He moved into lodgings in Main Street, Windermere, and took a job working in the kitchens of the Sutherland Restaurant at Bowness-on-Windermere.

With Ince's acquittal the Essex police were left with an unsolved murder. Most of the detectives believed at that time that it was the murderer who had been cleared: now they had an open file and no new leads. Had it not been for the strange happenings in the Lake District there is little doubt that the murder would have remained undetected.

But just three weeks later, on June 14, came a dramatic new development. Peter Hanson gave himself up to the Cumbria police. He knew the police were looking for him in connection with a break-in in Westmorland, and he decided to admit to the crime in the hope that he would be treated more leniently. While he was being interviewed by the police he told a fascinating story about a man named Brook. He talked about the gun his room-mate had shown him, described the shot he had heard fired, and recounted the conversation in which Brook had said that Ince would not be found guilty because he had not murdered Mrs Patience. He, Brook, had done it.

The police found Hanson's story extraordinary, but they had to check it out. They discovered where Brook was working and on June 15 Detective Constable Terry Crellin of the Kendal police went to the Sutherland Restaurant in Bowness and arrested him in the kitchens, on suspicion of possessing a firearm. Brook denied it. Crellin took Brook to Kendal police station and then went to his flat in Main Street, Windermere. After a thorough search of the room he found a slit in the mattress. Inside was the Beretta and fourteen rounds of ammunition.

The police confronted Brook with the Beretta. He admitted it was his, but refused to tell Crellin who had sold him the gun because, he said, his life would be in danger if he did. He would be done over. He did say, however, that he had bought the gun from friends in London just three days after he left Pentonville prison the previous October.

In fact, Brook had arranged to buy the gun when he was in Dartmoor. A prison officer had been constantly annoying him, and Brook decided that when he was released from prison he would get even with the man by shooting him. He had arranged to buy the gun through another prisoner he had met in Dartmoor, and when eventually he was released the deal went through smoothly. Brook was given a choice of three weapons by a dealer with whom he was put in touch – the Beretta, a Browning sub-machine gun, or a naval Colt. He decided on the Beretta; the others were too expensive. He had paid a £50 deposit in Dartmoor, which had been smuggled out, and he had paid another £50 to the contact he met after his release. He never named this man.

Brook dropped the idea of shooting the Dartmoor prison officer, but he kept the gun and carried it around with him. He told Crellin he had bought the gun with seventeen rounds of ammunition, and he had fired three of them. He had fired one shot when he bought the gun, to make sure that it worked, another when he thought the gun was getting rusty, and a third at the Salutation Hotel.

The Kendal police found the whole story quite plausible, particularly after what they had been told by Hanson. But was Hanson's claim that Brook had murdered Mrs Patience true? Essex CID were contacted and Detective Chief Superintendent Len White drove north with Detective Superintendent George Harris. The Beretta was sent to Nottingham for examination by ballistics experts. They compared the bullets used to shoot Bob and Beverley Patience with Brook's Beretta. The two matched. Brook's Beretta was the murder weapon.

Immediately the whole complexion of the case changed. The Essex detectives, who had been so sure that George Ince was the murderer, now had in their possession what they had never had through both Ince's trials – the murder weapon. Brook had admitted it was his, although he completely denied any involvement in the Barn shootings. During several long interviews with White and Harris, Brook said that on the weekend of the murder he had been staying with his grandmother in Leeds. He admitted that he had heard of Bob Patience, but said that he had never met him. He said that when he went to Leeds for the weekend he had left the gun in London.

At that stage the police were not in a position to charge him with murder. The evidence against him amounted to his possession of the gun and the claim by Hanson, who had a record of petty crime, that Brook had told him he had actually murdered Mrs Patience. It was mostly hearsay. The police realized that this time they would have to find the second man who had been in the Sun Lido House that November night. They examined Brook's past, searching for a possible friendship, a former criminal accomplice, any suggestion of a relationship which might have led Brook into taking the other man with him to the Barn.

It was not easy. Brook was a loner, a man who did not form close friendships. Although he had a long criminal record he had no regular criminal partners. He had never mixed with other prisoners in the various gaols in which he had spent so much of his life. But Harris and White began checking on every prisoner with whom Brook had shared a cell, following up every hint of even a casual acquaintanceship. The name of Nicholas de Clare Johnson emerged. Brook and Johnson had been together on the Pentonville prison hostel scheme; they had worked together; and there were signs that the two men had been friends.

Johnson's movements at the time of the murder were checked, and as his story unfolded he was almost dismissed as a possible suspect. While Brook had completed his sentence and been released on October 13, three weeks before the murder, Johnson had remained at Pentonville until the following January. That seemed to remove any chance that Johnson might have been the accomplice at the Barn. But when Essex detectives made a further check and examined the Pentonville records they discovered that, while it was certainly true that Johnson had another two months to serve at the time of the

Barn murder, on the weekend concerned he had been granted leave to visit a friend in Hampshire. He had signed out of the prison at 5 pm on Friday November 3, and signed back in again at 10 pm on Sunday November 5. So he could well have been in Braintree on the Saturday night. Further investigation showed that Brook and Johnson had first met some time before they were in Pentonville together, and that they had both been at Grendon Underhill prison, the psychiatric jail in Aylesbury, Buckinghamshire, several years before.

But where was he now? He had completed his prison sentence in January and had been released. Unknown to the Essex detectives Johnson was once again in custody. After his release he had worked for a while as a warehouseman. But the man who had spent so much of his life in prison, always for petty offences, mostly involving cars, was soon in trouble again. This time it was an indirect result of his friendship with Stanley Vane, the friend whose address he had left with Pentonville prison on the weekend he went to the Barn with John Brook.

Vane was a wealthy and philanthropic man, well known and liked in the Romsey area where he lived. He was middle-aged, retired, and a bachelor. He had first met Johnson at a fête in Broadlands, the Hampshire country home of the Mountbatten family, when Johnson was living in the area, and they discovered that they shared an interest in antiques, among other things. Vane found Johnson an open, friendly man and invited him to come and stay with him from time to time. Johnson sometimes referred to him as 'uncle'. Vane used to note the days when Johnson was coming to visit him in his diary, and one of the smaller points which led the Essex police to believe that Johnson had arrived at Vane's home on the Sunday after the Barn shootings was an entry in the diary which read 'Nicky returned'. The diary showed that it was Johnson's fifth visit; it was usual, the diary showed, for Johnson to arrive on a Friday. And on this occasion Johnson had, as we have seen, told the Pentonville prison authorities that he would be going straight to Romsey when he left prison on the Friday night. In fact he spent only the Sunday with his 'Uncle Stanley'.

After his final release from prison in January 1973 Johnson

went to stay with Vane. Vane was perfectly happy for him to take his girlfriends along as well, and Johnson often did. He did not tell Vane about himself, and it seems that Vane was not aware of his criminal record, or indeed that he was still serving a prison sentence when the visits began. Johnson had been staying with Vane for only a couple of weeks when Vane had to go into hospital for a minor operation. There were unexpected complications and Vane tragically died. Johnson, who had visited him in hospital, had been very worried by his friend's illness and upset by his death. He stayed on at the house for a while afterwards.

When he left he took Vane's car with him and a wallet containing £15. The local police had discovered this, and when the Essex police finally tracked him down he was on trial at Southampton Crown Court, charged with the theft of the car and the money and with driving while disqualified.

It was a difficult situation for them. Their interview with Johnson was bound to be speculative. In contrast with the case of Brook, the Essex detectives had no pressing reason to believe that Johnson was involved in the Barn murder. Nobody had mentioned his name, certainly not Brook. There was no evidence at all to point towards Johnson, merely the fact that he had known Brook, had been in prison with him and worked with him, and had been away from prison during the weekend of the murder. But it was clear that White and Harris had to talk to him, in the hope of establishing a firmer lead.

The Barn murder hunt had taken the police from Essex to Westmorland; now they went to Hampshire. Johnson appeared at Southampton Crown Court on Thursday June 21, to plead not guilty to stealing the Cortina and the money but guilty to the three charges of driving while disqualified. He was found guilty on the three driving charges and sentenced to nine months' imprisonment on each, to run concurrently, and was given a further six months for stealing the wallet and money. He was cleared of stealing the car. White and Harris were in court, and there they got their first look at the person they felt might be the second man in the Barn murder. His appearance fitted the rather vague description Beverley Patience had given them. She had concentrated on the gunman, but was able to recall that the second man was about six feet tall, had dark-brown hair, brown eyes, and hair just beginning to turn up at the back. It wasn't much to go on. Nevertheless, his appearance did not rule him out.

The Essex detectives sought permission from the local police and prison officers to talk to Johnson after the day's court hearing was over. This was granted. At that stage Johnson's trial was not over. The prosecution closing speech had been heard, but the defence counsel had still to sum up. White and Harris interviewed Johnson that evening in the Crown Court building. The interview lasted several hours.

At first Johnson denied knowing anything about the murder, but he soon cracked. White and Harris felt that he was very relieved to get it off his chest. He told them: 'Just charge me, I have had it on my mind for a long time. I have not been able to go to church because of it. Why do you think I have been ill?' Johnson told them he had got involved with a psychopath he couldn't control. He had had to stop work a couple of days after the murder because of illness. He had had very bad migraine and had been in hospital with hepatitis. On one occasion, he said, he had taken far too much codeine. He hadn't wanted to wake up the next morning.

Once he had admitted that he had been at the Barn on November 5 and that Brook had been with him and fired the shots, Johnson spoke freely, calmly and at length. He had clearly found it hard to live with the knowledge of his guilt, particularly when another man had been on trial for the crime. He had nearly confessed while the Ince trials were going on, he said. He told White: 'I was expecting you. I have dreamed about this. I'm not worried now. I am calm. I was a coward to let another man stand trial.'

He had had no idea, he said, that Brook was carrying a gun. The two men had gone to the Barn for a simple robbery, having heard that there was a great deal of money in the safe. But things had got out of control. Johnson had been afraid that he too would be shot, so he had had to convince Brook that he needed him. 'I feel now just as I felt when Ince stood trial. I do not want to see any man condemned to prison because of me. I should have stopped the case.' In his long conversation with the Essex detectives Johnson became worked up about only one thing: Bob Patience's behaviour on the night of the murder. He said he thought Patience was an incredibly stupid man not to have handed over the keys immediately.

White and Harris were not in an easy position. Every detective knows that confessions in themselves are not proof of guilt: criminal history is riddled with bogus ones. It is not unusual during murder trials for the police to receive confessions from members of the public claiming that they, and not the men in the dock, were responsible for the crime, and a jury will always be guided to ignore a confession. It can certainly provide the basis for further investigation, but not until the facts have been corroborated do they comprise a case against the confessor.

Nevertheless, White and Harris believed Johnson's story. It fitted in so many ways. There was detail in it, detail about the Barn and the Sun Lido House, about the break-in itself, which confirmed other evidence the police had, but which had at no time appeared in the press or come out at the Ince trials. There was certainly a solid basis for looking for corroboration.

There were two easily verifiable areas which if proved correct would almost confirm that Johnson was telling the truth. Both concerned the events after the murder, the retreat from Braintree. Johnson was specific in his description of what went on that night. He described how he and Brook sat down in a pillbox in the middle of a field to divide the spoils of their robbery. He said the bank bags had been buried and the cheques had been burnt. And he talked about the lift the two men had hitched in a Land-Rover with four Irish workmen, the bottle of milk they had bought off a milk float, the second lift they had hitched. The two detectives were amazed. Was it possible in all the blaze of publicity in the aftermath of the murder, when nobody could have failed to be aware that a massive murder investigation was being carried out around Braintree, that men who had given a lift to two bedraggled men, for it had been raining heavily very early in the morning after the murder, would not have come forward? It *was* possible. It had happened.

White and Harris left Southampton to return to their home territory. They were in the fortunate position of not having to make a sudden decision over charging, since Brook was anyway in custody in the north over the possession of the firearm and Johnson was serving a prison sentence in the south. Both men were safely under surveillance, and the Essex policemen could afford to take their time. But after the embarrassment of having their twice-tried suspect acquitted, having a seven-month-old unsolved murder on their hands, and now being reasonably sure that they were on to the right men this time, they wanted to wrap up the case as soon as they could.

First they checked the escape route from the Barn which Johnson had described to them. It was inevitably rather vague – it had been night-time, the two men were not familiar with the area, and they had walked across country. But there were specific details like the statement that they had walked along a railway-line, and that they had sat down for a while in a pillbox. Johnson had drawn a map for White and Harris. The detectives used it to retrace the route of the killer and his accomplice away from the Barn.

The disused railway-track was found, and was the first corroboration of Johnson's story. No railway-track had featured in any reports of the murder, or of the Ince trials. Secondly, they checked the method of entry to the house described by Johnson; that also indicated that he was telling the truth. The police had thought the intruders entered the Sun Lido House through a veranda at the front. Johnson said they went in through a rear upstairs window and remarked upon a teddy-bear he saw lying on the bed. It was Beverley's bedroom and the teddy-bear was hers.

But finding the pillbox proved difficult. Those who knew the area could not think of a building which fitted the description. There was a massive search involving dozens of police officers. Helicopters were brought in for an aerial search. Still the pillbox could not be found. Even the Assistant Chief Constable of Essex, William Petherick, joined in the search, and in the end it was he who spotted it. One Sunday afternoon, Petherick and Harris were walking over the area again, more on the off-chance of spotting something than by way of a concerted search.

They were about to pack up for the afternoon when Petherick noticed an overgrown stone building. They went inside.

It was in fact an old air-raid shelter at High Roding, seven miles from the Barn. The floor was dry earth. There were traces of burnt paper. Johnson had said that he and Brook had burnt the cheques while they rested there. Harris and Petherick dug into the loose earth and found the remains of two bank bags. It was now beyond doubt that Johnson had been telling the truth.

Through inquiries in the area the police came across three schoolboys who had done some digging in that same air-raid shelter many months before. They had unearthed a table cigarette lighter, a screwdriver and a bunch of keys. The lighter was identified by Bob Patience, though until it was shown to him he did not know that he had lost it. The screwdriver also belonged to Patience. The keys were Johnson's. He had been carrying a fairly standard car thieves' kit, twelve keys and a bootlace.

The police managed to trace the milkman who had sold Brook and Johnson a pint of milk each early on the morning of November 5, on the outskirts of Chelmsford. And they found the workmen who had given them a lift in their Land-Rover earlier that morning. The four labourers had been on their way to dig trenches when they were flagged down by two men who were soaking wet and said they had been to a party. The other man who had given Brook and Johnson a lift was never traced, despite newspaper appeals.

The Essex detectives were now convinced of the authenticity of Johnson's confession. A report was sent to the Director of Public Prosecutions: on August 1 Brook and Johnson were charged with the murder of Muriel Patience.

In December, when their trial had still not started, Johnson was in Wandsworth prison and Ince, recently convicted of the bullion robbery, was in the same prison. One day Johnson went up to him in the exercise yard and said he wanted to apologize for allowing Ince to go through two murder trials before making his confession. Ince looked at him in surprise, then replied simply, 'Fuck off.' Johnson scuttled away. It was their only meeting.

* * *

The trial began at Chelmsford Crown Court on Tuesday January 15, 1974, in the court next door to the one in which George Ince had been cleared of the murder. Mr Justice Stocker was the third judge to hear a Barn murder trial. John Leonard QC presented the case for the prosecution for the third time.

Two of George Ince's sisters, Betty and Margaret, were in the public gallery. Betty's husband George was there too. It was yet another indication of the way the Barn murder had taken over their lives. Their brother had been acquitted of the murder, and he was in prison beginning his fifteen-year sentence for his part in the Mountnessing hijacking. But somehow they couldn't leave the case alone, couldn't accept that the Ince family's part in it was over. They were drawn irresistibly to look at the two men whose silence had almost allowed their George to serve a life sentence. At least two of the Ince family were in court every day.

They knew through the East End grapevine that their brother's name was to be mentioned almost daily in the course of the trial and they felt that far from his innocence being proclaimed his name would in some way continue to be connected with the murder. The family had said repeatedly, from the day George was acquitted until the day the third trial started, that according to the books George had been cleared of the murder, but that was a very different thing from being declared an innocent man. The stigma was there, and it always would be. Before the Barn murder nobody had heard of George Ince. He was now a national name.

The family had heard that yet more allegations might be made against their brother during the trial of the new defendants. They were quite right. It was possible that the prosecution would go to great lengths not to mention Ince, but would concentrate on this trial in isolation. It was equally possible that any mention of Ince could be ruled out of order by Mr Justice Stocker as being irrelevant to this trial. Three factors weighed against this happening.

First, there was no chance that a jury could be selected which was unaware of the details of the case. Second, much of the evidence had been heard before; the same murder would be described and obviously the story couldn't change much. Third, many of the witnesses would be the same as in the previous trials.

From the moment the trial started, with not one objection being raised against any juryman (there was one woman in the jury), it was clear that again there would be no pretence that the other trials hadn't happened. In fact for one of the defence counsels it would be a major plank of his case. Mr Leonard had the onerous task of having to put as convincing a case against Brook and Johnson as he had twice tried to do against Ince. He came clean in his opening statement. The jury would be aware, he said, that there had been two earlier trials of a man called George Ince, and that the prosecution case in each of these had depended purely and simply on identification evidence, primarily that of the surviving members of the Patience family. They would be called again because they were the only people who could describe the events of that November night. But this time they would not be asked to try to identify the two defendants.

Mr Leonard had no alternative. Beverley had said from the witness-box that she was one hundred per cent certain that Ince was the gunman. She could hardly be expected to say now that she was one hundred per cent certain that Brook was the man. Mr Leonard was clearly speaking with feeling when he said: 'The Crown must accept that on the previous occasion the identification of George Ince by the Patience family was wrong. The Crown can no longer put the Patience family forward as witnesses upon whom you could rely on the matter of identification. Maybe it is all the better for that.' Nobody would have disagreed. Identification evidence had taken a heavy blow in the Barn case.

The first prosecution witness was Bob Patience, walking confidently into the court, once again dominating the proceedings. Oliver Martin QC, counsel for Brook, pinned his case on the fact that Ince had been positively identified as the gunman by two people who had spent a considerable amount of time in the room with him. He had little choice. Not only did he have to answer the prosecution's case, he also had to cope with Patrick Back QC, Johnson's counsel, who was defending a man who had confessed to being at the Barn on the night of the murder and had said he was there with Brook.

In effect three separate stories were being advanced by the three key barristers. First there was the prosecution case that Brook and Johnson had been at the Barn together, that Brook had fired the three shots, and that Johnson would hardly have been unaware that Brook had the gun and was therefore equally guilty of murder. Second, there was Johnson's case: that he had been to the Barn with Brook but had gone there for what he understood was a simple robbery; that he had not known Brook was carrying a gun; that he had been horrified and appalled when the gun was produced and the shots were fired; that he had stayed with Brook because he had the gun and he was frightened of him. In the words of Back, his counsel, he had been harnessed to a tiger. Yet his actions in trying to help Mrs Patience after she had been shot showed that he was the unwilling and unknowing participant in what turned out to be a murder. He had also claimed that he had already left the room when the shots were fired at Bob and Beverley Patience, and in fact he was not charged with the attempted murders of those two, but only with the murder itself. Thirdly, there was Brook's case. While admitting the gun was his, the basis of his defence was that he had lent it to Johnson and that he himself had not been at the Barn. Johnson had gone there with another man, and his counsel, Martin, implied most strongly that that man was George Ince.

Martin was the most extrovert and theatrical of the three barristers. He gave a series of stunning performances throughout the trial. He constructed a colourful scenario which involved Johnson, the bullion robbery and Ince. The one character who had no part in the drama Martin constructed was, of course, his client Brook.

Martin hammered away at the amount of money it had been admitted was in Patience's safe. How odd. How unusual to keep so much money there. Patience protested. He ran a busy restaurant and a popular nightspot. He featured a cabaret and the cabaret artists were expensive and liked to be paid in cash. It seemed, at times, as though Patience himself was on trial. He turned, in vain, to the judge in the hope that this line of questioning would be stopped, but Martin was allowed to go on.

Martin repeatedly said how odd the robbery was. 'If the object of the visit to your house was simply robbery it was a very peculiar kind of robbery, don't you think? There's your safe full of money and jewellery in a holdall and the so-called robbers walk off with two bags full of paper which contained only a small percentage of the money available in the safe. Doesn't that strike you as odd?' he asked Patience. Patience said that it did not. After the trial was over Patience was still fuming over what had been said about him. 'My name has been maligned and I have been accused of many things,' he said. 'I have had no right of reply.'

The trial was a much calmer affair than those which had gone before with Ince in the dock. There was the occasional outburst from Brook. His grandmother, who has a heart condition, collapsed in the witness-box while giving evidence and had to be revived by an ambulance man who was fortunately sitting in the public gallery. The only unexpected events came at the end of the trial. First, there was an anonymous phone-call to the wife of one of the jurors three days before the trial ended. The caller threatened violence if Brook was convicted. The call was followed by an anonymous letter threatening all the jurors, and as a result of this they were given police protection after they were discharged.

The jury was out for four hours. When it returned, the verdicts were as expected. Brook was found guilty of murder and guilty of two charges of attempted murder. He was given three life-sentences. Johnson was cleared of murder but found guilty of manslaughter. He was given a ten-year sentence.

But the drama was not over yet. A message was passed to the judge. There had been a telephoned warning that there was a bomb in the court. It was cleared for twenty minutes. While the court was empty and the building was searched Brook and Johnson were waiting in the room below the dock. A few moments before the adjournment ended Brook lunged at Johnson. There was a scuffle and blows were exchanged before prison officers dragged the men apart. They had been friends once, and partners in one of the most notorious crimes of recent years. One paper described them as the loner and the loser. The loner, aware that most of the rest of his life would be spent in prison as a result of the loser's confession, turned on his one-time friend in a last desperate attempt at vengeance. Like the robbery which gave Brook just £200 and turned him into a murderer it was a futile effort.

So fifteen months and three trials after Mrs Patience died the guilty men were sentenced. Justice, it would be said, had been done. The Barn murder file was closed, and as far as the courts and the police were concerned it was all over. But the investigations, questions, recriminations and post-mortems were still to come.

9 · A security leak

On November 29, 1973, six months after Ince was cleared of the Barn murder, four of the five men accused of hijacking a £400,000 consignment of silver bullion at Mountnessing, Essex, in May 1972, were found guilty at the Old Bailey. They were George Ince, Ronald Molloy, Frankie Sims and John Brett. Chic Matthews was acquitted. The judge, Mr Justice Milmo, told the four men that he was satisfied that each was a dangerous criminal. The robbery, he said, had been planned and executed with military precision. Sentencing them separately to fifteen years each he told them: 'You played for very high stakes – something over a third of a million pounds – and the penalty must be severe.' Ince held up his hand to speak. 'Sir, can I just say one thing please. . . .'

'No,' said the judge. 'Take him down.'

The cells at Brentwood police station are divided from the main administrative block by steel grille gates. If the prisoners are talking to each other from behind their cell doors the conversation can easily be heard in the passage by the grille. At about 7.30 pm on December 12, 1972, two new prisoners at Brentwood, Ronald Molloy and Chic Matthews, were chatting to each other. Detective Chief Superintendent George Harris, who had just finished interviewing Molloy, thought he might pick up some useful information and arranged for one of his Detective Constables to record what the prisoners were saying by putting a tape-recorder by the grille gates.

The early part of the conversation concerned the questionnaire that Molloy had just completed with Harris. He had taken it back to his cell to sign each page but had decided he didn't like the way he had answered some questions and was trying to flush one page down the toilet in his cell. Matthews, who was next to be questioned, wanted to know what it was like in the interview room and what they had asked him. Matthews said: 'Well, we just tell them the truth, that's it.' They were discussing where they had been on particular days and who they had been with and what they had done. After a short pause, Molloy said: 'It's a get-up, the ID, I'll tell you that.'

'Eh?' said Matthews.

'It's a get-up, the ID,' Molloy repeated.

'That's all right,' Matthews said.

'Well, we know that we've got our things, don't we?' said Molloy.

Why did the prisoners think the ID was a 'get-up'; what did Molloy mean by they would 'be all right because they had their things'; what were the 'things'?

During the court hearings that followed against Ince, Molloy, Matthews, Sims and Brett, an extraordinary story came to light. It emerged that nearly a hundred prosecution statements taken by the Essex police immediately after the robbery on May 2 had found their way into the hands of the suspects *before* they had even been arrested.

There had clearly been a major security leak, but its full implications were not made public either before or during the court hearings. Essex police claimed, after the final trial at the Old Bailey, that they had realized that copies of statements had been removed, either from the robbery 'incident' room at Brentwood police station or from the local Regional Crime Squad offices, some time between the end of May and the middle of June 1972 – within six weeks of the hijacking. But the police further admitted that the first real hint that they were in the hands of their suspects came during that conversation between Matthews and Molloy in the cells. It was then that they had figured out that 'things' must have referred to the statements.

The police did not know – and had not known during that summer – which of the defendants were in possession of which statements. It was a vital consideration: prosecution witnesses, including policemen, had described men they had seen running away from the robbery and would be asked to take part in the identification parades. If the suspects already knew what their descriptions were going to be, they were at a considerable advantage. But, more importantly, the police had to allow for the fact that the names and addresses of their witnesses were known to the suspects. By the time the court hearings began it was quite possible for some of those witnesses to have been contacted either by the suspects or someone acting on their behalf: for six months their witnesses could have been open to intimidation.

As we have indicated in Chapter 2, there was a crucial interview with the man known as Golly Sillett, who had been caught running away from the hijacking and had subsequently named Ince, Sims and Molloy as having taken part in it. Sillett had specifically requested that the statement which he eventually made should not include those names, for his own protection. The police agreed, but even the police record of the interview, which, of course had included the names, had found its way into the hands of the accused.

The full significance of the missing statements can only be seen when they are studied alongside those which the police finally produced for the prosecution evidence in the bullion trial. It is clear that the defence had been provided with a unique insight into the way in which the prosecution case had been constructed.

One of the most controversial aspects of the police identification of the robbers is the fact that several of the officers saw photographs of the accused *before* they picked them out on ID parades. In their statements the officers indicate that they saw the photographs quite accidentally. It is all the more disturbing for that very reason: if there is a long time lapse between the crime and the identification parade it seems almost inevitable that pictures of the suspects – circulated to police stations in the area – will be seen by the investigating officers. This becomes clear from an examination of the various statements.

Police Sergeant John Waddington, a driving instructor from the police headquarters at Chelmsford, was one of the first police officers to identify Molloy. On the day of the robbery he had joined in the general search for the stolen bullion truck. Waddington made his first statement about the robbery on May 3, the day after it had happened. The events which he described did not differ from those which he put into his final statement, made eight months later on January 17, 1973. He had received a radio message telling him that a container lorry had been seen in Wyatt's Green Road – in the general direction of Ongar from the Mountnessing roundabout. He drove along Wyatt's Green Road and came across the entrance to a farm on his left-hand side. Another policeman, in a dog van, was just ahead of him. Waddington recalled: 'Parked in the entrance-way [to the farm] was a grey 2/3 ton van with an index mark finishing with the letter C and with a male person in the driver's seat. I paused for perhaps a second or so, saw no other movement and not knowing the location of the abandoned container lorry decided to continue . . .'. A quarter of a mile further down the road Waddington found the abandoned container lorry. But at the same time, in his rear-view mirror, he saw the grey van that had been in the entrance to the farm drive off in the opposite direction. He gave chase but lost it in the narrow lanes.

It was then that he made a rough sketch of the man he had seen in the driving seat. The sketch was made on a scrap of paper attached to a clipboard on which he had been recording radio messages. 'I would describe the driver as 45–50 years of age, oval face, large nose and receding grey hair,' he wrote. The same day he gave a description of the man he had seen to another police officer who made up a Photofit.

After he had made up the Photofit picture Waddington was instructed by his senior officers not to read the *Essex Police Crime Information* which published photographs of the men wanted in connection with the bullion robbery. 'In fact, I tried not to see any publications,' he said, 'but about June 16 I saw the publication issued on that date and immediately thought that the photograph of the wanted man Molloy bore a close resemblance to the man I had made a Photofit impression of on May 3.'

Waddington was to see two more pictures of Molloy before he picked him out on an identification parade. The first was again in the *Essex Police Crime Information*, dated November 22.

'I was still of the same mind in respect of Molloy,' said Waddington. The second was the day before the ID parade on December 11. 'This would have been a fleeting glance of a newspaper lying open in the foyer of the police driving school,' he said. 'I did not pay particular attention to it as I was just walking through the foyer to join students who were waiting for me in a car outside the building.'

The following day, December 12, Waddington went on an ID parade for Molloy at Brentwood police station. He said afterwards: 'I identified Molloy and although he had brown hair whereas I originally said he had greying hair, I am reasonably satisfied that he is the same man. His facial features from the mouth upwards bore a close resemblance to the man I saw driving the van on May 2, particularly the protruding ears, boxer's nose and receding hairline.'

Two more policemen picked out Molloy on the December 12 parade. The first was PC A. J. Collinson. He had been on the search for the hijackers, accompanied by a police dog called 'Blue'. It was Collinson who had chased two men across an orchard, near Pilgrims Hatch, three miles from the Mountnessing roundabout, at about 2.45 pm; he had tried to catch them but they had stopped a Hillman car, pushed the driver out and made their getaway. Collinson had managed to get hold of one of the men. He described him as between 5′ 10″ and 6′, heavy build, light-brown hair swept back, fairly thin and receding at the front, clean-shaven with a high forehead and large ears. He said he was wearing a light woollen jumper with long sleeves, dark blue jeans and black Chelsea-type boots. He was covered in mud on the right sleeve of his jumper and his right leg from the knee downwards.

On May 9 Collinson made up a Photofit of the man who had got into the passenger seat side of the Hillman car. He spent a considerable time on it, but was not satisfied that he had compiled a good likeness of the man, particularly, he said, in respect of his eyes and his lips. About three weeks after the robbery Collinson saw a police circulation containing a photograph of Molloy. 'I immediately recognized him as being the person I had spoken to,' he said later. After that he saw two further similar publications including the same photograph of Molloy. On December 11 he saw the same photo again in the *Daily Mirror*. The following day he picked out Molloy on an ID parade at Brentwood.

The missing statements also make possible an analysis of the identification evidence produced, at various stages after the robbery, by each eye-witness. Such an analysis is now attempted. It is particularly interesting to note which of the witnesses makes an immediate description – that is in their first statements – of the man they say they saw, and, if not, how long after the event they finally pick out the suspect on an identification parade. Also, of course, what particular points of the original description fit that suspect. In the evidence from the police there is no suggestion that each officer did not follow the correct procedure and note the physical descriptions of the men they saw running away from the robbery immediately after they had seen them. What does emerge in some cases, however, is that these descriptions were not recorded in the officers' initial statements. Yet those officers knew that a very serious crime had been committed and they were taking part in a massive search for the robbers. The defence's discovery, from the missing statements, of these facts did not help the prosecution case.

PC Alan Kent was the officer who had chased and finally caught Golly Sillett as he was running away. Kent had been with PC Brian Ladd in an unmarked patrol car on the Ongar Road when he saw four men come through a hedge on to the main road. He had timed the incident at about 3.05 pm. Ladd was driving and had stopped the car near the men on the opposite side of the road. In his first statement about the events that followed, made on May 3, Kent did not give any descriptions of the men; he simply retold in detail how he had caught Sillett when he had slipped in some mud. Sillett, of course, was his main concern at the time.

Kent made another statement on December 21 – a full seven months later and nine days *after* he had picked out Molloy as one of the men who was running away. (It is, of course, standard procedure for witnesses who have identified suspects on parade to make such statements.) In Kent's December statement he said that as he had got out of the car the faces of the four men had been clearly visible. He had not seen any police circulations containing photographs of suspects until November 28, when he had received a 'personal circulation concerning the persons wanted in connection with the hijacking'. On this he had recognized two of the four men whom he had seen in Ongar Road on May 2. One of them he 'seemed to recognize' was Ronald Molloy. On December 11, he saw Molloy's picture in the *Daily Mirror* and again recognized him as being one of the four men. The next day he picked Molloy out on an ID parade at Brentwood. 'I cannot be absolutely sure, but I am reasonably certain he was one of the men,' said Kent after the parade. 'His height, age and general facial features were the same as that of one of the persons I saw, in particular his receding hair line, protruding ears and thick lips were distinctive.'

That concluded the police identification of Molloy. But he had also been positively identified by the security guard of the bullion truck, Raymond Kerley. In his original statement on May 5 Kerley described only two men in any detail. The first was the man who had come to his side of the cab of the truck and ordered him out, the second the man with a gun who had told Tony Evans, the driver, to get out. Kerley had not described anyone looking like Molloy, but when he saw him on the ID parade he picked him out. 'I did not get such a good look at this man as I did of the man standing right beside the door, but I had a good picture of his face in my mind and in particular his nose which was broad and solid looking,' said Kerley after the parade. Kerley admitted that two days before the parade – on December 10 – he had seen the 'Police Five' programme during which a picture of Molloy had appeared.

George Ince was identified by two of the policemen who had identified Molloy – PCs Kent and Collinson – and also by the driver of PC Kent's car, PC Brian Ladd. Collinson, it will be remembered, had first seen the two men walking across the orchard near Pilgrim's Hatch, and had followed them to Ash Close, where they got into the Hillman car. Collinson identified the man who got into the passenger seat as Molloy, but he also identified the man who pushed out the woman driver and then drove the car away. That was Ince, he said. In his first statement, on May 3, Collinson described him as between twenty-five and thirty years old, about 5′ 9″ to 5′ 11″, wearing a light-coloured shirt and blue jeans.

When Collinson saw the first police circulation (about three weeks after the robbery) containing the photographs of Ince and Molloy he did not feel sure about Ince. But he saw two further publications with the photo before picking out Ince on the ID parade at Colchester on November 29. He said afterwards:

'After asking each man on the parade to turn round once I recognized one of the two men who I chased across the fields . . . into Ash Close on May 2, 1972. This was the same man who shortly afterwards hijacked a Hillman Minx Saloon from Ash Close. I only had a fleeting glimpse of this man's face that afternoon, however I am reasonably satisfied that this was the first man that ran to the car from his overall build, height, colour of his hair and general appearance from side and rear which I studied closely on the parade.' In his original statement Collinson had not described the overall build or the hair colour of the man he finally said was Ince.

The identification of Ince by PCs Kent and Ladd is similarly interesting. Their car had pulled up on the opposite side of the Ongar Road from where they had seen four men about to climb through a hedge. Kent, as has been said, confined his first statement, on May 3, to retelling how he had caught Sillett. In a further statement, made on December 21, he recalled that as he got out of the car the faces of the four men were clearly visible. One of the men, he said, was more forward than the rest: 'He was in fact, most of the way through the hedge.' Nearly seven months after the robbery he recognized this man as George Ince when he looked at the police circulation which had been dropped in his tray on the morning of Tuesday November 28. Next day, on the ID parade at Colchester police station, Kent said: 'I immediately recognized Ince and positively identified him as the man who was more forward than the rest on May 2.'

PC Ladd got out of the car at the same time as PC Kent, but did not get a good view of all the men coming up to the hedge. 'But,' he said in his statement on December 21 (he did not make one before that date), 'one of the men was further forward than the other three and was partly through the hedge when he saw us. I had a good view of this man.' Ladd stayed with the car to radio for assistance, then gave chase, but did not see any of the men again – apart from Sillett.

Ladd was told by senior officers not to look at police circulations concerning the incident and did not see a photograph of any of the men until November 29, when, like Kent, he received a personal issue circulation with Ince's picture on it. 'I recognized the man George Ince as one of the four men I had seen at Ongar Road, Pilgrims Hatch on May 2,' he stated confidently. 'This was the man who had been slightly in front of the other men and partly through the hedge. There is no doubt in my mind about this.' At 4.50 pm that afternoon he identified Ince on an ID parade.

No civilian witnesses identified Ince, and only Kerley, the security guard of the bullion truck, had identified Molloy. But according to the dog handler, PC Collinson, both Ince and Molloy had gone into Ash Close, where they had made their getaway in a Hillman car.

There were two civilian witnesses to this event. One was the driver and owner of the car, Mrs Ivy Asker, who had jumped out as the hijacker revved the engine. As she had got out, another man jumped in – according to PC Collinson, this was Molloy. Watching this performance was a builder's labourer, Francis Sargeant, who was working on extensions to two houses in Ash Close. All three, PC Collinson, Mrs Asker and Mr Sargeant, had roughly equal opportunity of seeing the distinguishing features of the two men. Collinson was the only one to identify them on ID parade.

PC Collinson said that Ince was twenty-five to thirty, about 5′ 9″ to 5′ 11″, wearing a light-coloured shirt and blue jeans.

Mrs Asker said the hijacker was aged thirty-five to forty, 5′ 8″ to 9″, stocky build, brown hair of conventional length but very dishevelled at the time, fresh complexion. He was dressed in a dark shirt with either short or rolled-up sleeves. She could not describe his trousers or shoes, except that they must have been very muddy because of the amount of mud left in her car.

Francis Sargeant only saw the man from the back but he thought he was about 5′ 10″ tall, had a reasonable head of brown hair, was in his late twenties or early thirties, was fairly powerfully built and was wearing a grey jacket.

Collinson described Molloy as about thirty-five to forty years of age, height between 5′ 10″ and 6′, heavy build, light-brown hair swept back, fairly thin and receding at the front, a high forehead, clean-shaven with large ears. He was dressed in a light-blue woollen jumper with long sleeves, dark blue jeans and black Chelsea-type boots. He was covered in mud on the right sleeve of his jumper and his right leg from his knee downwards.

Mrs Asker said the second man she saw was of medium height, about 5′ 8″ to 9″, thirty to forty years old, of medium build. She recalled he was wearing a dark shirt. She did not think she would be able to identify this man.

Francis Sargeant said that the man was about six foot tall, wearing a grey cardigan or a woolly shirt, dark trousers and winklepicker type boots. 'He was limping; walking on the outside of his right foot. He was thin, long faced and there was something on his face, I couldn't make out if this was a beard or dirt. He had long black straight hair, this was all over the place when I saw him. They looked like a couple of gypsies.'

Frankie Sims was identified by Detective Constable Kenneth Foster and Raymond Kerley, the security guard. He was also picked out by a policewoman who had seen him with Sillett

Incident at Ash Close

Suspect	*Witness*	*Age*	*Height*	*Hair Colour*	*Facial Features*	*Build*	*Clothes* *Top*	*Bottom*	*Shoes*
INCE	PC ANTHONY COLLINSON	25–30	5′ 9″–5′ 11″	—	—	—	Light-coloured shirt	Blue jeans	—
	MRS IVY ASKER	35–40	5′ 8″–5′ 9″	Brown (dishevelled)	Fresh complexion	Stocky	Dark shirt, short sleeves	—	Muddy shoes
	FRANCIS SARGEANT	25–35	5′ 10″	Brown	—	Powerful	Grey jacket	—	—
MOLLOY	PC ANTHONY COLLINSON	35–40	5′ 10″–6′ 0″	Light brown fairly thin swept back	High forehead, clean-shaven, large ears	Heavy	Light-blue woollen jumper	Dark-blue jeans	Black Chelsea boots
	MRS IVY ASKER	30–40	5′ 8″–5′ 9″	—	—	—	Dark shirt	—	—
	FRANCIS SARGEANT	—	6′ 0″	Long black straight	Long-faced	Thin	Grey cardigan or woolly shirt	Dark trousers	Winkle-picker boots

on the day of the robbery. Foster and Kerley gave similar descriptions of Sims. Foster said he had passed a car being driven by Sims on a stretch of road near Wyatt's Green on May 2. Sims, he said, had appeared to be between thirty and thirty-five, thick-set with brown hair. Kerley said it was Sims who had brandished an iron bar at him as he was sitting in the cab of the bullion truck just after it had been hijacked. He described Sims as aged thirty to thirty-five, about 5′ 10″ or 11″, heavy build but not fat, very ruddy complexion, with a fattish face.

Both descriptions fitted Sims. But there was a curious incident during cross-examination of Foster's evidence. It gave the police their second hint that original prosecution statements were in the hands of the defence. Foster was asked if he had an earlier statement than the one tendered in evidence – after all that had been written on January 12, eight months after the robbery had taken place. 'I did not make an earlier statement about these events,' said Foster. 'I do not know why I did not make an earlier statement.' Sims's counsel was somewhat taken aback. In his hand he had a copy of a statement made by Foster dated May 30. The description he had given of Sims on May 30 was actually the same as he had given on January 12, almost word for word, but why this lapse of memory? Foster later admitted that he had, in fact, made the earlier statement.

There was no identification evidence against John Brett or Chic Matthews, although both were put on parades. (Brett's alibi was that he had been picketting in a union strike at the Royal group of docks. Matthews did not give evidence.)

The trial of these five men began at the Old Bailey on September 4, 1973, and finished sixty days later, on November 29. Superintendent Harris said he considered that the inquiry had been a classic police investigation, carried out exactly to the book. He did not think any of his men would have lost a moment's sleep over anything they had done. Mr Montague Waters QC, for Ince, saw it differently. In his closing speech he said that there was evidence that the police had shown an excess of zeal. Certainly, apart from the extraordinary affair of the missing statements, the trial was notable for a number of allegations made against the police.

There was, for instance, the case of Billy Lampon, to whom Ince had lent his car. Lampon, a Hackney borough council engineer, appeared in court as a prosecution witness but during the course of his evidence the Crown had successfully applied for him to be declared hostile. He had said that a statement he made about how he actually came to be in possession of Ince's car had been forced out of him by the police. Lampon claimed that during questioning his ears were banged, he was punched in the stomach, stripped and his head banged against the wall. He said he suffered bruises on his head, back and face and he had a black eye. He had gone straight to a doctor for an examination after he was released and to a photographer's studio. Mr Waters said that the prosecution could have checked with the doctor and the photographer, but they did not. There were other allegations of the police asking for statements to be changed and of evidence being planted.

Allegations of this kind are not uncommon: indeed, of the allegations made in this trial Mr Justice Milmo said: 'One of the least fortunate aspects of this trial is that all sorts of allegations and suggestions have been bandied about. But virtually none of them have been put to the police officer so that he could answer these allegations.' After the trial the judge called the Assistant Chief Constable of Essex, Mr William Petherick, before the court, and asked him to convey to his Chief Constable his commendation of the police officers involved in the case.

The judge also praised the milk roundsman, Owen Whymark, who had hindered the getaway van by driving his milk float in front of it. 'When he recognized a crime was being committed, with great presence of mind he did not stop his vehicle at once but drove straight to the nearest telephone, with the result that the police were able to raise hue and cry within minutes. If it had not been for that it is at least doubtful whether these men would have been caught. If members of the public could always be relied upon to act in that manner in similar circumstances there would be fewer major criminals escaping justice today.'

Whymark had indeed made every effort to help the police, and the defendants knew it. From the missing statements they were aware that he had told the Essex police on the day after the robbery that he was unable to give any description of the men involved and that he would not recognize them again. They knew Whymark had repeated that in a further statement on May 9. 'I saw that the driver's door was open and I saw two men drag the driver from his cabin,' he told DC Connolly. 'At this time I was about twenty-five yards away from the incident and I viewed this through the open side of my float. I got the impression that both of the men were in shirt sleeves. I could not see what they did with the driver once they got him out. I am unable to give a more detailed description of the two men.'

The Essex police decided, however, that Whymark should be shown two of the suspects. On November 29 he was taken to Colchester police station to see if he recognized Ince on an identification parade. He did not. On December 6 he was taken to Brentwood police station to see if he recognized John Brett. He did not.

For all the men, apart from Matthews, the police had found scientific evidence linking them with the robbery. Handwriting experts testified that a series of applications for registration of the vehicles used in the robbery had been made, in false names, by the defendants. Brett's thumbprint was found on the van abandoned on the A12. It was this van which had been used to stop the bullion lorry. In Sims's car the police found a globule of silver on a jacket.

Nevertheless, the main weight of the police case had rested on the identification evidence, and, rather more ponderously, on the circumstantial evidence that when the men had been living together, in the Margate hotel and at the caravan site, they had been free spenders. After a summing-up from Mr Justice Milmo which lasted for seven long days the jury came to the conclusion that the police identification evidence was to be believed beyond reasonable doubt.

It was not, of course, the end of the case. The four men immediately announced that they would be appealing. There was also an immediate inquiry into the missing statements;

senior officers from the West Yorkshire Metropolitan Constabulary were appointed to investigate how these had been made available to the defence. Their inquiry was continuing at the time of writing.

10 · Identification and the law

'What is the use of going through the farce – the monstrous farce – of an identification parade when the witness has been shown photographs of the suspect before he is identified?' – Mr Dummet, Bow Street Magistrate, 1936.

WHEN Roy Jenkins was made Home Secretary in the new Labour Government at the end of February 1974 he had already earned a reputation as a reformist. Within a month of his taking office two important cases of wrongful conviction became headline news and Jenkins reacted immediately. Luke Dougherty and Lazlo Varig had been wrongly imprisoned for nine months and five years respectively as a result of identification evidence which was later shown to be false. Even before the row over their convictions had reached its peak Jenkins set up a committee to look into the whole question of identification.

The committee had no brief to inquire into the case of George Ince – that was already being dealt with by an internal police inquiry, and in any event Ince had been acquitted. But it is fair to say that his case had added considerably to the pressure that was mounting on the Home Office to do something about false identifications. Ian Mikardo, the MP for Poplar who became chairman of the Parliamentary Labour Party after the election, had taken a close interest in Ince's case and was instrumental in ensuring that the police inquiry was set up. He wrote many letters to the Tory Home Secretary, Robert Carr, about the case and had told the Ince family he would not be satisfied until an independent inquiry team had looked into the Barn murder investigation.

On April 9 Jenkins told the House of Commons about the

committee he was setting up. The case against Mr Varig, he said, rested on identification evidence:

> On the face of it this was substantial – he was picked out on properly conducted identification parades by no less than eight witnesses, three officers of the Gloucestershire police, two officers of the Liverpool police and three civilian witnesses. However, a number of witnesses did not so identify him and it is now apparent that those witnesses who did were most unfortunately mistaken.
>
> The case of Mr Dougherty has already given cause for concern about the efficacy of identification procedures and there have been other cases where doubts have been felt. I am convinced that this is an area of the criminal law and police procedure which needs urgent review, and I have therefore appointed a small committee to examine it, in the light of Mr Varig's and Mr Dougherty's convictions and of any other relevant cases.

Lord Devlin was appointed to head the committee. It was a popular appointment; Devlin, a former judge, has headed a number of important committees of inquiry, including that of the port transport industry. The other members appointed to the committee, which was still sitting at the time of writing, were: Mrs John Freeman, a member of the Overseas Welfare Committee of the Save the Children Fund and wife of the former Ambassador to Washington; Mr David Hopkinson, editor of the *Birmingham Evening Mail* and a member of the committee inquiring into contempt of court; Mr Jeremy Hutchinson QC, a Recorder and a member of the Committee on Immigration Appeals; and Mr P. D. Knights, former Chief Constable of Sheffield, now Chief Constable of South Yorkshire.

The setting up of the inquiry was welcomed by Sir Robert Mark, Commissioner of the Metropolitan Police. It was right, he said, for the public to be concerned over a wrongful conviction; such convictions undermined public confidence in our system of justice. If the police, the lawyers and the courts did their jobs properly the most likely cause of wrongful conviction was mistaken identity. Most policemen, he said, were sympathetic to demands for a higher standard of proof when identification was the most important issue. Authoritative legal observers were publicly thankful that the Devlin committee's brief was a wide and imprecise one: it allowed them to consider the matter of identification in the broadest way. But many solicitors were unhappy that they were not represented on the team. After all, solicitors, as a group, have extensive first-hand experience of ID parades.

Luke Dougherty was sentenced to fifteen months' imprisonment for stealing three pairs of curtains worth £11·25 in Durham in August 1972. At the time of the theft he was on a coach trip with twenty other adults and some children. He had been identified by an assistant manager and a supervisor in the shop where the curtains had been stolen. The police had shown a series of photographs from the criminal record office to these two men and they had picked out Dougherty, who had a criminal record. This identification was the only evidence offered against him. Two of the passengers on the coach on which he was travelling were called to give alibi evidence. The jury rejected their testimony in favour of the other evidence.

Dougherty appealed and asked for other members of the coach party to be allowed to provide alibi evidence. But the appeal judges said that since these other people were available at the time of the original trial their evidence was not new, and consequently could not be allowed. The case only came back to appeal in March 1974 because it had been taken up by Tom Sargant, the tireless legal watchdog who is secretary of Justice, the British section of the International Commission of Jurists. When the appeal was finally upheld and Dougherty was released Lord Gardiner, Justice chairman and former Lord Chancellor, felt it appropriate to speak out on identification procedures. Most wrong convictions were on the matter of identification, he said. In particular, the use of photographs by the police raised questions, he said, because no one could be sure what the police said to witnesses as they examined the photographs.

Police procedure over identification in the Dougherty case

had been shown to be at variance with the rules: both the key witnesses for the prosecution had been allowed to look at photographs and had picked out Dougherty from the pictures. If the recommended procedure had been followed one of them would have been shown the photographs and the other would have been a witness to an identification parade in which Dougherty was the suspect. Dougherty never went on an identification parade.

The Varig case was more disturbing because there the recommended procedure had been followed. Varig had been sentenced to ten years' imprisonment in Gloucester in 1969 for various offences in Liverpool including using a firearm to resist arrest and wounding a police officer with intent to cause grievous bodily harm. He appealed against conviction, but this was rejected in 1970. It was only later, when similar offences had been committed in London, that it seemed likely that the man who had committed those was the same man responsible for the offences for which Varig had been found guilty. The office of the Director of Public Prosecutions decided that Varig's case should be investigated. As a result of the inquiry the Home Secretary gave Varig a free pardon and he was released from prison on April 5, 1974. He had served five years.

Varig had been picked out on identification parades by eight people, five of them policemen, the rest civilians. The fact that all these eight people were later shown to be wrong, as several people were shown to be wrong in identifying Ince as the Barn murderer, once again challenged the credibility of identification evidence. Did it have any validity at all as a means of proving guilt?

The first case of mistaken identification to be seriously investigated was that of Adolf Beck in 1896. Beck was sentenced to seven years for fraud; he served five years of the sentence before being released and granted a free pardon. He had been identified positively by ten different people, but the frauds were later discovered conclusively to be the work of another man who resembled Beck – William Augustus Wyatt.

The next turning-point came in 1925, when a Horse Guards officer, Major R. O. Sheppard, was wrongly arrested for a petty burglary. He was identified by the owner of the property which had been entered. There was much moral indignation at the summary treatment this officer received from the police and there followed a full-scale Home Office inquiry. Importantly, it concluded that other prisoners besides Major Sheppard must have been similarly treated.

Major Sheppard was identified hurriedly and late at night when, as the Home Office report said, it must have been very difficult to find men of similar appearance. The whole system of police identification was remodelled after the Sheppard affair with three main reforms: first, that the suspect should be placed on parade with a number of others of as far as possible, similar height and general appearance, and that no intimation of the identity of the accused should be given to the eye-witnesses; second, that the suspect should have the right to stand anywhere in the parade; third, that the suspect was entitled to have a solicitor present during the parade.

The new guidelines considerably increased the police's workload: finding men of similar appearance meant that identification parades took up much more time. Early in 1926 one newspaper reported the difficulty police had encountered when they had picked up a black suspect. A search was made of the East End. Some of the black men were scared when the detectives asked them to come into the station for a few minutes. The same report continued: 'Ten men wearing light grey overcoats and soft hats were wanted for an ID parade in West London. Detectives found them all in one restaurant at lunchtime.'

There is certainly a persuasive argument that the human memory for faces is so fallible that evidence of identification is virtually worthless. An interesting experiment was conducted in the form of a television programme called 'The Evidence of Your Eyes', shown early in 1974. A series of tests involving a studio audience were carried out by Laurie Taylor, a lecturer at York University who is a student of identification. A murder was re-enacted on stage and then members of the audience were asked detailed questions about what had taken place. They were asked who had done what, how many shots had been fired and what had been said. A large number of the answers were wrong. The murder was acted out again, in slow motion, and then the 'murderer' was put on an identification parade so that members of the audience could pick him out. More than half of them picked out the wrong man.

When it is remembered that this was a staged event – the audience had not happened to be passing the scene of a crime but were concentrating their attention on the crime being carried out in front of them on stage – the implications of so many people being wrong are horrifying. It seems likely that most people are quite incapable of remembering a face.

Two artificial means have been devised to assist the eye-witness to portray his recollections of the physical appearances of a suspect in picture form. The first, known as the Identikit, was introduced to Britain from the US in 1961. It was developed by a Los Angeles detective, Hugh McDonald, in the 1940s. After taking thousands of pictures of faces he reduced all human types to 52 chins, 33 pairs of lips, 102 sets of eyes, 32 noses, 80 eyebrows and 126 hairlines. From these he calculated that 62 billion faces could be made up. The kit consists of line drawings of facial features on transparent slides which, when put together on the instructions of the witness, make up a face.

The first man to be caught in Britain by this method was an Anglo-Indian, Edwin Albert Bush. He was walking in a Soho street on March 7, 1961, when PC Hilton Cole recognized him from an Identikit picture of a man who was wanted for the murder of a woman who had been stabbed to death in an antique shop. Bush was found guilty and was later hanged.

One of the more controversial cases in which the Identikit method has been used is the A6 murder. James Hanratty was found guilty of the murder of Michael Gregsten in February 1962 and was hanged two months later. Two Identikits were issued from descriptions given first by Gregsten's girl-friend, Valerie Storie, and then by another man who saw somebody in a car pass nearby the scene of the crime. Hanratty's trial judge, Mr Justice Gorman, said in his summing up that he had 'no view about how much use these pictures are'. Since Hanratty was hanged there have been many doubts cast about his guilt; another man, Peter Louis Alphon, has publicly confessed to the murder. Until July 1974, when Roy Jenkins appointed a QC to investigate the whole affair, the Home Office have always appeared reluctant to re-open the case, mainly, it seems, because Alphon does not fit the description of the killer that was current at the A6 trial. In particular his eyes are hazel and Storie had been struck, so she told the court, by the killer's 'very large, pale blue, staring icy eyes'.

But the description of the killer put out within twelve hours of the murder was for a man with brown eyes. It remained part of the official description for four days, but according to the police the brown eyes feature did not come from Miss Storie. The Identikit picture she made up three days after the murder, however, contained not pale and icy eyes, but extremely dark ones. A *Sunday Times* reporter, Lewis Chester, took Miss Storie's original Identikit picture to Hugh McDonald, in California. He told Chester: 'I have reconstructed the Identikit portrait which was composed with Miss Storie, from my own kit here in this office. Although the photocopies I have seen do not mention the codings used for the original assembly of this portrait, I would judge that the code E49 was probably used for the eyes. E49 is the code for very dark eyes.' The evidence was with the Home Office at the time of writing.

In 1970 a completely new system came into operation. Called Photofit, it was developed by Jacques Penry, a former door-to-door Bible salesman, who had been trying to get the system accepted by British police forces for twenty years. Unlike the Identikit process, which used line drawings, Photofit depends on actual photographs of hairlines, eyes, lips, ears and chins to build up the complete portrait. There are 5,339,210,240 variations of the face. This was the system used by the Essex police in both the Barn murder hunt and the inquiry into the Mountnessing bullion robbery.

The evidence against George Ince in the Barn murder was purely and simply identification. The one piece of additional evidence, the fibres found on his coat, was discredited. The case against him in his two trials amounted to the fact that several people picked him out from photographs and on identification parades. Two of these people had spent some considerable time close to the gunman in the room in which the shootings happened.

Beverley Patience was said to be a good witness. Both judges, Melford Stevenson and Eveleigh, remarked upon this. She had spent about half an hour in the room with the gunman. She had been positive about the photographs shown to her. She

Identification Parades for Barn Murder

I. FOR IDENTIFICATION OF ALLEGED GUNMAN

Suspect	*Witness*	*Suspect identified?*	*Another identified?*	*Comments*
First parade – Nov. 27, 72	Beverley Patience	Yes	—	—
	Bob Patience	No	Yes	Later changed mind. Said he should have picked Ince.
INCE	David Patience	Yes	—	At first said not certain. Later said 100% certain.
	Jonathan Ridley	No	No	—
	Bunny Layzell	Yes	—	—
Second parade –	Harry Leverett	Yes	—	Said: 'I think it is this man.'
Nov. 29, 72	Arthur Lewis	No	No	—
INCE	Renée Jarvis	No	No	—

2. FOR IDENTIFICATION OF ALLEGED ACCOMPLICE

Suspect	*Witness*	*Suspect Identified?*	*Another identified?*	*Comments*
First parade – Dec. 5, 72	Beverley Patience	No	Yes	Identified A
	Bob Patience	Yes	—	Walked length of line four times
	David Patience	No	Yes	Identified A
JOHN BRETT	Bunny Layzell	No	Yes	Identified B
	Harry Leverett	No	Yes	Identified B
	John Pickering	No	Yes	Identified A
	Mrs Lund	No	Yes	Identified A
Second parade – Dec. 14, 72	Beverley Patience	No	Yes	Identified L
	Bob Patience	No	Yes	Identified L
MR X	David Patience	No	No	—
	Harry Leverett	No	No	—
Third parade – Jan. 24, 73	Beverley Patience	No	Yes	Identified M
	Bob Patience	No	Yes	Identified M
	David Patience	No	Yes	Identified N
MR Y	Bunny Layzell	No	Yes	Identified P
	Harry Leverett	Yes	—	
	Joseph Ripton	No	Yes	Identified S

had gone straight up to Ince on the identification parade and picked him out. At first sight this appears convincing, but Beverley's record throughout all the identification parades in which she took part tarnishes this view. She went on a total of four identification parades; one for the alleged murderer, Ince, and three for the alleged accomplice. She picked out Ince on the first parade. But on the three parades for the three men who were suspected of being the accomplice, John Brett and two others, she also picked out somebody – on each occasion an innocent member of the public voluntarily taking part in the parade.

On no occasion did Beverley pick out the suspect, fortunately, since the suspect was in each case also innocent. But Beverley's identification performance, looked at in the context of four parades, is not impressive. Four parades; four identifications; one identification of the suspect. This, it might be thought, would have reduced the reliability with which she could be considered as a prosecution witness.

Bob Patience's performance, similarly analysed, is no more impressive. He had spent some twenty minutes with the gunman and his accomplice. He also attended the same four parades as his daughter. As we have seen he did not pick out Ince, but later changed his mind and said he had meant to. He picked out John Brett in the second parade, and on the third and fourth parades he picked out innocent members of the public. His record runs: four parades; four identifications; two identifications of the suspect (one on second thoughts). He approached the whole affair with customary zeal: after picking out Brett as the gunman's accomplice he then went on two more parades and picked out two more men, also as the gunman's accomplice.

David Patience caught a fleeting glimpse of the two men as they drove away from the Barn. He picked out Ince on the first parade, initially saying he was not positive but later changing this to say he was completely sure. On the other three parades for the gunman's accomplice he made identifications on two occasions. Each time it was an innocent member of the public. David Patience's record runs: four parades; three identifications; one identification of the suspect (not certain at first, but later certain).

The ID parade for John Brett, even superficially examined, was a farce. Seven witnesses were asked if they could pick out the gunman's accomplice from the line. Only Bob Patience picked out Brett, but every witness at the parade made a positive identification. One man, an innocent member of the public making up the parade, was identified four times.

* * *

In 1969 the Home Office reviewed the advice given in the old circulars of 1925, and issued a new memorandum. We have already dealt with its basic instructions for the conduct of identity parades in Chapter 5 and the memorandum is reprinted in full in the Appendix. We shall attempt here to relate some aspects of the inquiries into the murder and the bullion robbery to the memorandum.

One of the most important of the new instructions concerned the use of photographs of suspects. There were three general points. First, photographs should never be shown to witnesses for the purpose of identification if a personal identification is possible. Second, where the use of photographs is the only way of tracing a culprit, a witness should be left to himself to make a selection from among a number of similar photographs. Third, if one witness makes an identification in this way, other witnesses should be asked to attend an identification parade.

The new memorandum did not satisfy Justice in respect of the recommendations on photographs. They proposed that it should be an 'absolute rule that photographs are shown to a witness only to bring in a suspect and that witnesses attending a parade should be given no assistance, either by way of photographs or descriptions'. Justice noted that when the Criminal Law Revision Committee reported on identification evidence in 1972 the inherent dangers in the use of photographs were recognized but no proposals made to minimize them. The committee went so far as to suggest that there is no need for an identification parade after a witness has 'positively' identified a suspect from a photograph. But it made no reference to the Scottish practice of only showing photographs to one or two witnesses and introducing the remainder to ID parades.

The rules for the showing of photographs is of particular significance in both the murder and the bullion investigations. The dangers are inherent from the start: all policemen know the care with which the photographs must be presented to the witnesses; no help must be given in picking out a suspect. There has been no suggestion that Essex police performed this part of their duties with anything but exemplary fairness. It seems to the authors, however, that the procedure then adopted – of showing not one but several witnesses pictures of the suspect – was in contravention of the 1969 memorandum.

During the investigation into the Barn murder Beverley Patience was first shown a picture of George Ince while she was still recovering from her wound at the Black Notley Hospital. On November 10, Detective Chief Inspector Wyatt first showed her the card of twelve pictures, with Ince at No. 3. She picked him out. Immediately afterwards he showed the card to Bob Patience. He picked out Nos 6 and 8. According to the book, Bob Patience should not have been shown the pictures. The suspect had been identified by the main eyewitness and at that stage it was the police's task to find him and present him to other witnesses on an ID parade. As we know, the police visited Ince's two known haunts in London the following day, November 11, without success.

A week later, November 18, Beverley was again shown the card of twelve, and again picked out Ince. But she was also shown a selection of four pictures of him taken, he claims, without his knowledge a year previously when he was in a police station for questioning about a café brawl. Finally, she was shown a fifth picture taken ten years earlier in 1962. (That was the picture of Ince kept in the files of the Criminal Records Office, which had been taken when he had been sentenced to two years' corrective training for stealing £9 12*s* from the till of a TV shop.) On being shown the fifth picture, Beverley, according to Wyatt, sat upright in bed and positively identified Ince. On November 24 Wyatt showed yet another picture of Ince to Beverley; she studied it through a magnifying glass and positively identified Ince again. So after her initial identification from a photograph she was shown seven more pictures of Ince on two separate occasions.

After Beverley's initial identification several other people saw pictures of Ince. Raymond Hawkins, the customs officer, and Bunny Layzell, the lorry driver, were shown the card of twelve. But pictures of Ince were shown after he had been arrested; Hawkins was shown one and so were the two Felsted schoolboys who had told the police they had seen two people who fitted the descriptions of the raiders in the village shop. One of the boys said he positively recognized Ince.

In the bullion trial the most obvious deviation from the procedure laid down in the 1969 memorandum concerned the identification of Ince by PCs Kent and Ladd. Police circulations containing pictures of Ince had been dropped in their trays on the morning before in the case of Kent, and on the same day in Ladd's case, that they picked him out on ID parades. On both occasions it was after Ince had been arrested.

Another controversial point of identification evidence has always been the amount of information put before the jury about the difference, if any, between the appearance and physical characteristics of the suspects identified and the descriptions given in the witnesses' original statements. Justice's evidence to the CLRC on this point said that these differences usually become known to the jury, either through the fairness of the prosecution or through cross-examination. But it was not always the case. 'It should, therefore,' said Justice, 'be the rule that descriptions given are recorded, signed by the witness, and automatically made available to the defence.'

Again the evidence of PCs Kent and Ladd in the bullion trial is worthy of scrutiny. Kent picked out Ince and Molloy; Ladd only picked out Ince. And yet neither made any description of either man in their first statements, six months earlier, about their part in chasing the men who were running away from the scene of the hijacking. Kent had said after the parade that Molloy's height, age and general features were the same as that of one of the persons he saw; in particular his receding hair line, protruding ears and thick lips were distinctive. Ladd said he immediately recognized Ince from the photograph, and that there was no doubt in his mind. Raymond Kerley, the security guard, picked out Molloy, but he had made no description of Molloy in his first statement.

The CLRC was particularly concerned about the amount of evidence of this kind which should be made available to the jury. They suggested that, by means of an administrative direction, the police should be asked to supply the defence with copies of descriptions of the offender which any likely witness had given them. They thought it desirable that a witness should be asked to write down or dictate his description as soon as possible – and before being shown any photographs. Justice approved of their recommendation but saw it as of 'little guaranteed value' unless the judge was specifically required to comment adversely if the procedure were not followed.

One of the main issues that the Devlin committee will be considering covers that last point. The question is not really one of changing the 1969 memorandum in any radical fashion but of devising means of encouraging the police to follow it. At present they are only advised. The National Council for Civil Liberties has favoured a solution where the procedures are made statutory. Another way is for the courts to reject all identification evidence in cases where the procedures have been disregarded. But some would like to adopt the American practice whereby cases in which the procedures are shown not to have been followed are simply thrown out.

If it is decided to rely simply on the warnings given by the judge these should be quite specific, as Justice has pointed out. For example, the honesty of the witness is seldom in doubt, but the validity of his or her testimony may well be. David Patience only had a fleeting glance of the man in his Volkswagen car as he was running from the Barn restaurant to the Sun Lido House on the night of the murder. Raymond Hawkins saw some people in a car, but he was tired, it was dark and he was driving past them at the time. Sergeant Waddington saw the man in the van in the entrance to Wolf's Farm for a split second or two – he too was driving. It seems to the authors that a person who has said in his first statement that he would not recognize the men again should not be called as a witness on an ID parade. Yet Owen Whymark, the milkman, said just that and he was called.

Justice has felt that the danger of wrong conviction is increased by a tendency of some judges to minimize the dangers of identification evidence in their summing up. 'Thus,' they say, 'a hesitating identification by one witness is sometimes fortified, while the evidence of alibi witnesses is denigrated – and defence counsel's references to Adolf Beck rebutted.'

* * *

There is one final issue which does not necessarily come within the scope of the Devlin committee but which, if police adherence to identification rules is tightened, must be considered. It is the present refusal of the Court of Criminal Appeal to interfere in any cases where there is evidence of identification which had been accepted by the jury. The Donovan Report on the Court of Criminal Appeal emphasizes that the right of appeal affords no protection to an accused unfortunate enough to be wrongly convicted in such circumstances. In the case of Ince and other mentioned in this book such protection is of signal importance.

Postscript

'I wouldn't like to take a chance on identifying anyone. You know what I think of identification parades' – George Ince at the committal proceedings for the man accused of attacking him with a knife in Long Lartin prison.

GEORGE INCE began his fifteen-year jail sentence in Wandsworth prison in south London, still protesting his innocence of the bullion robbery. The appeal was delayed while the various inquiries were being carried out. The one defendant in the bullion trial who was acquitted, Chic Matthews, said when he walked out of the Old Bailey a free man that the four who were convicted were his friends and he intended to prove their innocence.

Ince was made a Category A prisoner, maximum security, which meant that special precautions were taken over his incarceration and those who wanted to visit him were carefully screened by the Home Office. He was treated as a dangerous prisoner, a security risk. The night before the jury in the third Barn murder trial retired to consider their verdicts on Brook and Johnson, Ince was moved from Wandsworth to Long Lartin prison, near Evesham in Worcestershire. This is a modern prison, recently upgraded to maximum security, which has all the electronic surveillance equipment and computerized locks which make escape a near impossibility. Alsatian dogs patrol the perimeter, and floodlights mounted on high towers illuminate the prison at night.

Ince's transfer from Wandsworth to Long Lartin was carried out in the manner traditionally reserved for high risk prisoners. It took place in the middle of the night; a high-speed motorcade rushed him from London to Evesham while most people slept. By the time Brook was sentenced to life imprisonment three times over and taken to Wandsworth to begin his sentence Ince was already safely installed in a cell more than a hundred miles away. He was then taken off Category A, which meant he was free to have more visits. Mrs Grey was his only visitor: when he sent out visiting orders, naming the people he wanted to visit him, he never included his sisters. His family has never been altogether happy about the relationship, but they know he cares more for her than for anyone else.

After Brook's conviction Bob Patience spoke out for the first time about Ince's prosecution and his family's positive identification of Ince. He was satisfied, he said, that the right man had been convicted and justice had been done. And he apologized to the Ince family.

'I only hope that he [Ince] and his family will forgive the mistake,' the *Daily Express* reported him as saying. 'George Henry Ince was not the man who did the shooting. We all offer him our sympathy for putting his freedom on the murder charge at jeopardy and subjecting him to what must have been two torturous trials. All we can do is hope that he and his family will forgive the mistake. We know how they must feel.'

He went on to offer his interpretation of how the mistake had been made:

> I suppose we were just too close to the investigation and we may have heard things that we shouldn't have heard. Don't forget that at one time the police used the Barn as a base and it was impossible not to know what was going on. People may have said things innocently which probably registered. Although no one told me to pick Ince out, his name was being gossiped about and all of us now recall that we went into one room where Ince's picture was lying face upwards on a table. We were all anxious that my wife's shooting should be avenged, but not at the expense of an innocent man. After we saw Brook in the court we all agreed that he was a dead ringer for George Ince. Those same high cheekbones, steel blue eyes and the same receding hairline. Although we were not given a chance by the court to identify Brook or Johnson from the dock we are now absolutely sure that they were the men who were at the Barn.

Beverley Patience was more confused. When she went on the identity parade for Ince, she told the same paper, a lot of things were happening around her: she was frightened, she said, and she made a mistake.

A month after he had been moved to Long Lartin Ince had his face slashed. He was in the exercise yard watching a football match with a group of prisoners when there was a scuffle and he suddenly reeled back, blood streaming from his face. Prison officers immediately overpowered another inmate who was taken away to solitary confinement. The incident prompted more talk of vendettas and gangland feuds; it was related to the earlier attacks on Ince. In fact it seems more likely that some prisoner was trying to make a name for himself. Ince said later that his assailant had muttered something about him getting all the publicity. Prisoners like Ince whose names become well known often attract resentment and sometimes physical assault.

But once again it had been shown how accident-prone Ince was.

After the convictions of Brook and Johnson the Chief Constable of Essex, John Nightingale, ordered an investigation into allegations and complaints made by Ince over his prosecution for a murder he did not commit. There was great pressure on Nightingale to hold such an inquiry. Through his sister, Betty Cornwell, Ince had sent a letter listing all his complaints to his Member of Parliament, Ian Mikardo, who raised the matter with Mark Carlisle, then Minister of State at the Home Office. The outcome of this activity at a high political level was an inquiry under Section 49 of the 1964 Police Act. Under this Act all inquiries into complaints against the police are carried out by other policemen, in more serious cases by officers from a different force from that under investigation. Mikardo wrote to Mrs Cornwell that he would not be satisfied until there was an independent inquiry by someone from outside the police force, but he was prepared to wait until the inquiry ordered by Nightingale had been completed. A top-ranking Scotland Yard officer, Commander Emlyn Howells, was put in charge of the inquiry. He interviewed many people connected with the case – Essex police officers, members of the

Ince family and Mrs Grey among them. At the time of writing he was still conducting his investigations.

On March 7, 1974, he went to Long Lartin prison to interview George Ince himself. The interview lasted from 11.15 in the morning until 4.25 in the afternoon, and Ince said later that he was impressed by Howells's thoroughness. Ince made and signed a long statement, describing how and why he gave himself up when he heard he was wanted for the murder, his experiences after his arrest – his interrogation and identification parades – and making a series of allegations against the Essex police. He ended his statement: 'I did not murder Muriel Patience. I did not shoot Beverley and Bob Patience. I have never been in the Barn restaurant or the Patience home. I was wrongly charged and maliciously prosecuted. I have been acquitted of this charge after two trials during which me and my family went through hell and I want those responsible for this wrong prosecution to be dealt with.'

Soon after Easter 1974 Charlie Kray was released from Maidstone prison on parole. He had been a model prisoner and was eligible for maximum remission of sentence. He said he found it remarkable that some people thought of him as a villain. 'A lot of nonsense has been talked about me; people saying, for instance, that I was a gangster, so help me. I have never hurt anyone in my life.' He was allowed four days' short home leave, given at the the Home Office's discretion to prisoners nearing the end of their sentences and intended to help them adjust to the outside world before the final release date. Kray made more of it than most – it was one of the best publicized paroles of all time. Early one Friday morning he walked out through the prison gates, dressed smartly in a black leather coat and white turtle-neck sweater, and through an amusing coincidence he arranged to go and stay with a friend in St Mary Cray, Kent. His first message for the outside world was that his marriage to Dolly was over. Asked how he reacted to the news that she was having an affair with George Ince, he told the London *Evening News*: 'Well, I must be honest, I was absolutely shocked, numbed. As for now, it's over. It had to be that way; it's the only thing that can possibly happen.' He saw Dolly during the weekend leave and they both agreed that there was nothing left in their marriage and divorce was inevitable. Kray said he would remain friends with his wife because that was the most civilized thing to do.

When the weekend was over and Kray had returned to prison to serve the last few months of his sentence, Dolly felt able to admit publicly for the first time that the marriage was over. She went further: George Ince was the man she loved, she said, and she was going to marry him. An East End local reporter telephoned Ince's mother Minnie to ask what she thought about her son marrying Dolly. 'Over my dead body,' she said.

In April Ince was in court yet again – in Evesham, near Long Lartin prison. This time he was a prosecution witness. The man accused of slashing his face was in the dock. Ince made the short journey from Long Lartin prison to the court in an armoured police van accompanied by police cars and outriders, and security at the country court was tighter than it had ever been.

Ince was asked if the man in the dock was the one who had attacked him with a knife. He answered quietly and briefly, making in his own way the final comment on his experiences as the supposed Barn murderer. 'I wouldn't like to take a chance on identifying anyone,' he said. 'You know what I think of identification parades.' There was just a suggestion of a smile on his face.

Appendix - Home Office Circular No 9/1969

Identification Parades

1. The object of an identification parade is to make sure that the ability of the witness to recognise the suspect has been fairly and adequately tested.

2. Identification parades should be fair, and should be seen to be fair. Every precaution should be taken to see that they are so, and, in particular, to exclude any suspicion of unfairness or risk of erroneous identification through the witnesses' attention being directed specially to the suspected person instead of equally to all the persons paraded.

Conduct of identification parades

3. If an officer concerned with the case against the suspect is present, he should take no part in conducting the parade.

4. Wherever possible the officer arranging the parade should be of not less rank than inspector.

5. Once the identification parade has been formed, everything thereafter in respect of it should take place in the presence and hearing of the suspect, including any instructions to the witnesses attending it as to the procedure that they are to adopt.

6. All unauthorised persons should be strictly excluded from the place where the identification parade is held.

7. The witnesses should be prevented from seeing the suspect before he is paraded with other persons, and witnesses who have previously seen a photograph or description of the suspect should not be led into identifying the suspect by reason of their recollection of the photograph or description, as for instance by being shown the photograph or description shortly before the parade.

8. The suspect should be placed among persons (if practicable eight or more) who are as far as possible of the same

age, height, general appearance (including standard of dress and grooming) and position in life. If there are two suspects and they are of roughly similar appearance they may be paraded together with at least twelve other persons. Where, however, the two suspects are not similar in appearance, or where there are more than two suspects, separate parades should be held using different persons on each parade.

9. Occasionally all members of a group are possible suspects. This may happen where police officers are involved (e.g. an allegation concerning a police officer which can be narrowed down to a number of officers who were on duty at the place and time in question). In such circumstances an identification parade should not include more than two of the possible suspects. For example, if there were twelve police officers on duty at the time and place in question, there should be at least six parades, each including ten officers who were not implicated and not more than two who might have been: the twelve possible suspects should not be paraded together. Two suspects of obviously dissimilar appearance should not be included on the same parade. Where police officers in uniform form an identification parade, numerals should be concealed.

10. The suspect should be allowed to select his own position in the line and should be expressly asked if he has any objection to the persons present with him or the arrangements made. He should be informed that if he so desires he may have his solicitor or a friend present at the identification parade.

11. The witnesses should be introduced one by one and, on leaving, should not be allowed to communicate with witnesses still waiting to see the persons paraded; and the suspect should be informed that he may change his position after each witness has left.

12. The witness should be asked whether the person he has come to identify is on the parade. He should be told that if he cannot make a positive identification he should say so.

13. It is generally desirable that a witness should be asked to touch any person whom he purports to identify; but when the witness is nervous at the prospect of having to do this (as may occur when, for example, the witness is a woman or child who has been the victim of a sexual or violent assault or other

frightening experience) and prefers not to touch the person, identification by pointing out may be permitted.

14. If a witness indicates someone but is unable to identify him positively, this fact should be carefully noted by the officer conducting the parade, as should every other circumstance connected with it, whether the suspect or any other person is identified or not.

15. It may sometimes happen that a witness desires to see the suspect with his hat on or his hat off, and there is no objection to all persons paraded being thereupon asked to wear or remove their hats. Sometimes again there may be something peculiar in the suspect's gait or tone of voice, and if the witness desires to see the person walk or to hear the person speak, there is no objection to the person paraded being asked to walk or to speak. When any such request is made by a witness, the incident should be recorded.

Identification parades in prison

16. If the suspect is in prison and is willing to take part in an identification parade, arrangements should be made with the governor for his production at the nearest convenient police station where the parade may take place. A parade should be held in prison only if special security considerations make it unwise to hold it outside or the suspect refuses to take part in a parade unless it is held in prison.

17. Where a parade has to be held in prison, the governor will be responsible for the assembly of the parade and a prison officer will be present throughout in charge of the discipline of the prisoners taking part. A police officer, unconnected with the case, will otherwise be responsible for the parade (including the introduction of witnesses to the parade and the noting of all that takes place). He must ensure that the parade is conducted in the same way as a parade outside prison.

Use of photographs in identifying criminals

18. Photographs of suspects should never be shown to witnesses for the purpose of identification if circumstances allow of a personal identification. Even where a mistaken identifica-

tion does not result, the fact that a witness has been shown a photograph of the suspect before his ability to identify him has been properly tested at an identification parade will considerably detract from the value of his evidence.

19. Any photographs used should be available for production in court if called for.

20. If a witness makes a positive identification from photographs, other witnesses should not be shown photographs but should be asked to attend an identification parade.

21. Where there is other evidence identifying the accused with sufficient certainty to prefer a charge, a witness who has made a firm identification by photograph should not normally be taken to an identification parade. There may however be circumstances when it is desirable to ask the witness to identify the suspect from a parade. For example, identification may have been made from a poor or out-of-date photograph; the photographic identification may have been made so long previously that the present ability to identify is uncertain; the suspect's appearance may have materially altered since the photograph was taken; or the witness may think his identification is likely to be assisted by having an opportunity of hearing a suspect speaking or observing his gait. The decision whether a witness should, in such circumstances be taken to an identification parade should, wherever possible, be made by an officer of not less rank than inspector.

22. Where there is no evidence implicating the suspect save identification by photograph, the witnesses as to identification should be taken to an identification parade notwithstanding that they may already have made an identification by photograph.

23. The police should inform the defence of any case where an identification is first made from photographs since it cannot normally be said in court that an identification was made from photographs without revealing the existence of a criminal record.

24. Where it is necessary to show a photograph of the suspect, it should be shown among a number of other (unmarked) photographs having as close a resemblance to it as possible, and the witness should be left to make a selection without help and without opportunity of consulting other witnesses.

Index